THE BOOK THAT'S SWEEPING AMERICA!

THE BOOK THAT'S SWEEPING AMERICA!

Or
WHY I LOVE BUSINESS!

STEPHEN MICHAEL PETER THOMAS

As told to John Butman
The Consultant's Consultant

JOHN WILEY & SONS, INC.

New York • Chichester • Weinheim • Brisbane • Singapore • Toronto

Copyright © 1997 by John Butman.
Illustrations copyright © 1997 by Glenn Palmer-Smith
and Pamela Prichett.

Published by John Wiley & Sons, Inc.

Library of Congress Cataloging-in-Publication Data:

Thomas, Stephen Michael Peter.
    The book that's sweeping America! or Why I love business!
    Stephen Michael Peter Thomas.
        p.   cm.
    ISBN 0-471-17398-3 (cloth : alk. paper)
    1. Business — Humor.   I. Title.
PN6231.B85T48   1996
818'.5402 — dc20   96-36654

Printed in the United States of America

10 9 8 7 6 5 4 3 2 1

Contents

Explore leadership styles!

Learn teamwork skills!

Improve cross-cultural communications!

Shorten product development cycles!

Improve on-time performance!

Minimize gender differences!

Justify major expenditures!

Welcome!

The Book That's Sweeping America! is a breakthrough business book. Why? Because in this deceptively slim and easy-to-read volume, Stephen Michael Peter Thomas — The World's #1 Business Guru — explains the most powerful global business concepts. He offers results-oriented, easy-to-implement methods and practices. He draws on his years of experience as adviser to the world's most successful business organizations to provide you with knowledge, insight, and, yes, wisdom.

> **And yet, absolutely none of his ideas are actually new or different enough to challenge you or make you feel uncomfortable in any way.**

That's why so many Fortune 500 executives, influential government officials, academic heavyweights, and superstar athletes seek him out. Steve tells them exactly what they've heard a thousand times before, but makes it sound excitingly fresh and new.

Lee Iacocca,
legendary auto executive,
cites the Smeaton-Thomas
Success Factors Grid
as a significant factor
in maximizing his
leadership performance.

Now you can take advantage of Steve's decades of experience. He renders complex ideas so simple that virtually anyone can understand them — including your average CEO — through the innovative use of:

☛ Fascinating case **stories** and **interviews** drawn from the world's most successful organizations.

☛ Eye-catching **photos, charts,** and **graphics,** including Steve's own inimitable **drawings** and **visual "impressions."** (Call 1-888-4-STHOMAS.)

☛ Learning **summaries,** informative **Q&As,** and **exercises** you can implement in your workplace — tomorrow!

And, It's *Interactive*!

And that's not all. *The Book That's Sweeping America!* is the very first interactive business book. All the words have been individually selected and then carefully sequenced into user-friendly phrases, easily digestible sentences, and paragraphs crammed with powerful meaning.

> *However, the editors are keenly aware that no single word ordering is likely to meet the specific needs of every individual reader. Accordingly, the words and sentences can be read in any order you choose!*

Unlike other business books, *The Book That's Sweeping America!* does not force you into a rigid structure based on logic or on some personal creative or literary need of the author. No, *The Book That's Sweeping America!* allows you to explore the world of business at your own pace and in your own way — with absolutely no impact on the validity or coherence of the ideas.

So, let's begin!

In *The Book That's Sweeping America!*, you will join Stephen Michael Peter Thomas on an incredible journey into some of the world's most successful and progressive organizations.

You will meet visionary leaders.

You will encounter thought-provoking concepts.

William Gates,
well-known software executive,
attributes much of his
worldwide success to the
use of Global Hand Gestures
and Facial Expressions.

And, when you are done, you will find yourself inspired and motivated. You will return to the workplace eager to employ the fresh buzzwords and cleverly repackaged homilies you have just learned — without any fear they will have any impact whatsoever on your company, your colleagues, or the way you do business.

In fact, *The Book That's Sweeping America!* is so wonderfully obvious and incredibly basic you'll find it hard to believe that's all there is to it. But remember: Many of the world's most successful and influential people have paid astronomical fees to hear Stephen Michael Peter Thomas say even less than he does in this book.

And, now — in your own small way — you can be one of them!

The Editors

ow I Began This Life of Learning

Good Morning!

Thank you for joining me in this book.

Notice I did not say "my" book because *The Book That's Sweeping America!* truly is the work of many people. And so, before we begin Learning, please allow me to acknowledge, with a deep sense of humility and gratitude, a few of my collaborators:

☛ Thank you, **Clients!** You are among the most successful, brilliant, and influential people the world has ever known. It is possible that I have Learned almost as much from you as you have from me.

Client and friend
Margaret Thatcher,
as she departs from a three-day
Thomas seminar on minimiz-
ing gender differences in
the workplace.
(Call 1-888-4-STHOMAS.)

☞ Thank you, **Family!**
- Beloved parents
- Devoted wife
- Nine children (Hi, you Overachievers!)
- Faithful dog "Asset"

☞ Last, but not least, thank you, **Mr. Ray Wilson!**

☞
*My early
business mentor,
Mr. Raymond Wilson,
proprietor of
Wilson's Fish Market.*

My First Learnings

My first and most powerful Learnings were taught me by a humble — yet strangely effective — fish market proprietor, Ray Wilson.

You see, I was not always the globe-trotting confidante of tycoons, billionaires, and opinion leaders that I am today. No, I began as an average upper-middle-class boy, raised in an average affluent suburb completely free of crime or economic distress.

One high school summer, I took a job at Wilson's Fish Market in the island resort town where my parents owned a modest eight-bedroom brick mansion formerly owned by a world-famous whaling captain.

This being my first professional position, I was eager to perform competently, so I prepared for the job by reviewing the works of the seminal writers on business — beginning with Niccolò Machiavelli and continuing right up through Alfred P. Sloan Jr. — whose *My Years with General Motors* was then a hot seller.

Armed with this knowledge (which I suspect surpassed that of the average Fortune 500 CEO of the day), it was obvious from the moment I stepped in the door that Wilson's Fish was not much of a business. Why?

☛ We were at the downstream end of an unreliable supply chain. (Fish.)

☛ All corporate knowledge and memory, such as it was, resided in Mr. Wilson's brain. Despite his habit of scribbling notes on scratch pads and fish wrap strewn throughout the shop, a lot of important information fell through his mental cracks.

☞ The workplace smelled — and not in a fresh, saltwatery-fish way, but in a we-need-to-clean-the-fridge-more-often way.

Even so, Mr. Wilson was reasonably successful, thanks to a natural ability to focus on the customer (gabbing with them as he sliced into a haddock or popped open a clam) combined with a knack for cultivating his upstream supply partners (although the nightly imbibing with local fishermen that this required represented a significant expense item).

I saw, however, that Wilson's Fish had tremendous, unrealized potential. By redefining our mission, organizing for breakthrough improvement, and reengineering our core processes, we had the opportunity to shift our paradigm and virtually reinvent the Fish Market Industry, as it then was known.

And so, one evening when Mr. Wilson returned from an off-site conference (venue: Duffy's Tavern), I presented to him my Five-Year Plan for Wilson's Fish. It called for a program of change and improvement culminating in an IPO within two years, followed by worldwide expansion that would generate sufficient cash for Mr. Wilson to retire to Tarpon Springs by the age of 52.

Mr. Wilson eagerly agreed, and the next day a New Era began at Wilson's Fish. Up went a sign in the window:

(Courtesy: Mr. Raymond Wilson)

I redesigned our organizational structure and redefined our competency models. Here is the org chart I sketched on a sheet of fish wrap:

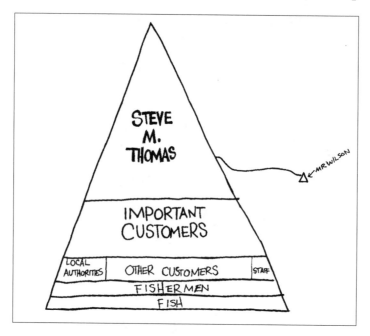

(Courtesy: Fish & Seafood News)

I initiated an extensive program of Learning — inviting vacationing members of various oceanographic, ichthyological, and business institutions to visit Wilson's Fish on an informal basis to keep us abreast of new knowledge in fish and fish management. Honorariums were paid in beer and slightly outdated cooked shrimp.

Within a month, my many efforts began to pay off:

☞ Impulse purchase of high-margin items such as codfish cheeks and cocktail sauce jumped by 36 percent.

☛ Board of Health citations plummeted by 48 percent.

☛ Staff productivity skyrocketed by 117 percent, enabling Mr. Wilson to spend more time on long-neglected strategic issues, such as tidying up the storage shed out back.

So successful were we that — by the end of the summer — the leading trade publication, *Fish & Seafood News*, named Wilson's Fish as Seafood Retailer of the Year, 1963. Mr. Wilson was thrilled by this honor. He begged me to join his permanent staff. He offered a substantial increase in salary and promised a piece of the action within three years. I thanked him but said I felt obligated to enter the tenth grade and complete my formal education.

I will never forget that summer. Indeed, the lessons learned during those few weeks of hard work and intense fishy aroma have shaped my entire professional life:

☛ Running a fish market (ergo: any business) isn't really that hard.

☛ At the same time, business management isn't so easy that you'd want to spend your whole life doing it.

☛ Good presentation skills, a modicum of knowledge and plenty of high-level "strategy talk" can make you as much money — and possibly lots more — than long hours and hard work.

I sensed there must be many businesses that weren't that hard to run and there must be many people running them who were ignorant of the business fundamentals. I thought: Perhaps I can devote my entire life to making dazzling presentations of extremely obvious ideas to business people, borrowing their ideas if they have any, and getting huge fees and recognition for doing it!

It seemed too good to be true — but that is exactly what I have done for more than two decades now!

So, I reserve my deepest thanks for my earliest teacher and business mentor — and the man who still supplies me with finest quality picked lobster meat — Mr. Ray Wilson.

THANK YOU, for getting a young boy started on this wonderful life of Learning!

Stephen Michael Peter Thomas

THE FIRST LEARNING

LEADERSHIP IS HARD

*"What is the difference
between a Leader and a Manager?*

*A Leader typically enjoys a controllable but
difficult-to-diagnose mental disorder.*

A Manager typically enjoys Golf."

STEPHEN MICHAEL PETER THOMAS

he Smeaton–Thomas Success Factors Grid

What differentiates the true Leader from the mere Manager? For many Leaders the most important difference can be summed up in these words: The Smeaton-Thomas Success Factors Grid.

The Success Factors Grid is a deceptively simple little device employed by the great majority of the Leaders of the world's most successful organizations, and I delight in taking some small credit for developing this essential Leadership tool.

My inspiration for The Grid came from the memoirs of a British engineer, John Smeaton, who was tasked in 1756 with rebuilding the Eddystone Lighthouse, which overlooks the English Channel. Smeaton developed what he called The Gridde to define the most important characteristics of the cement that would be used in construction.

Study it carefully:

Concerning Ye Success Propertys of Ceymentt

	Ruff	Smooth
Harde	Harde & Ruff	Harde & Smooth
Softe	Softe & Ruff	Softe & Smooth

(Courtesy: The Cement Foundation)

As you can see, each axis represents a Success Factor (X = smoothness, Y = hardness). The four possible combinations of the two factors form four **Quadrants.**

The upper right Quadrant represents the optimal combination of the two factors. In this case, Smeaton and his construction team sought to create cement surfaces that were both "Harde & Smooth."

The lower left Quadrant, of course, is the worst-case scenario: "Softe & Ruff" cement that might lead to structural weakness — and that today could easily result in a ruinous law suit.

When I first came across the Smeaton Gridde, I instantly sensed that it could be of use to the business Leader of today. But not, of course, in the crude state acceptable to a British engineer of the 18th century. So I enlisted the help of a team of specialists in information mapping and graphic design to refine and adapt Smeaton's original grid.

Here is the Thomas version, showing the business success factors that drive most business organizations today:

Business Success Factors

	Bad	Good
Fast	Fast & Bad	**Fast & Good!**
Slow	Slow & Bad	Slow & Good

I'm sure you can see that the new version (now generally referred to as The Thomas Grid), although owing some slight debt to the Smeaton version, bears very little resemblance to it.

Let's take a moment to analyze the four Quadrants of The Thomas Business Success Factors Grid:

Lower Left Quadrant: Slow & Bad

This is the worst-case combination, and such a business will only survive if:

☞ There is no competition within 10,000 miles.

☞ There is no need to make a profit.

Examples of such organizations include any utility or government agency. Perhaps the finest example of a successful Slow & Bad business is Howard Johnson's, which prospered for decades by employing the "oasis strategy" — siting their restaurants on desolated stretches of divided highways.

Upper Left Quadrant: Fast & Bad

It is possible to survive in this Quadrant, especially if your company operates in one those industries where speed is valued over quality:

☞ Rock & roll music.

☞ Car windshield replacement.

☞ Undertaking.

Lower Right Quadrant: Slow & Good

Many organizations can prosper in this Quadrant, but few can achieve growth. Here you will find, for example, most skilled craftspeople —

including carpenters, plumbers, poets, gardeners, and chefs in five-star restaurants.

Upper Right Quadrant: Fast & Good!
In this Quadrant, you will find the most successful organizations, most powerful Leaders, and, of course, the majority of my clients.

The beauty of The Thomas Grid is its flexibility. It can be applied to virtually every organization, department, discipline, and core process. Here, for example, is The Thomas Grid for New Product Development:

New Product Success Factors		

Lo-Price	Lo-Price & Lo-Quality	**Lo-Price** *&* **Hi-Quality!**
Hi-Price	Hi-Price & Lo-Quality	Hi-Price & Hi-Quality
	Lo-Quality	**Hi-Quality**

The Thomas Grid can be employed equally effectively by individuals to help define their own personal success factors. Here, for example, is The Thomas Grid of a well-known television talk show host:

Personal Success Factors

	Homeless	Billionaire
Slim	Slim & Homeless	**Slim** *&* **Billionaire!**
Heavy	Heavy & Homeless	Heavy & Billionaire

As an interesting aside, I have found that The Thomas Grid can even be used to determine the Success Factors that will create a best-selling business book such as the one you are now reading:

Business Book Success Factors

	Clever	Self-Important
Obvious	Obvious & Clever	**Obvious & Self-Important!**
Subtle	Subtle & Clever	Subtle & Self-Important

Subtle & Clever

You might think that Subtle & Clever would be the winning combination for any book. But our research (and, indeed, our personal experience) proves that no Subtle & Clever business book ever has been — and never could be — a best-seller.

Why? Because a Subtle & Clever text requires careful reading, and everyone knows that careful reading — in fact, reading of any kind — is just not possible in today's fast-paced, highly competitive global business environment.

Obvious & Clever

This combination will also fail. Why? Because it is physically impossible to be both Obvious & Clever at the same time. Accordingly, the text will have to alternate between being Obvious and being Clever. The reader with a keen appreciation of the Obvious will become confused and disoriented during the Clever parts. The Clever reader will be disgusted with the Obvious sections.

The result: Early remaindering.

Subtle & Self-Important

Sometimes a Self-Important consultant will team up with a Subtle writer to create a business book. The contempt the two will inevitably feel for each other will ooze from the pores of the page and turn most readers off.

Obvious & Self-Important!

This is the winning combination, as a survey of every successful business book in the past decade proves. How do we define *successful*?

- ☛ More than 100,000 copies in print.
- ☛ More than 10,000 of those copies purchased by people other than the Author and his/her associates.
- ☛ Lecture fee of $20,000 or more for the author.
- ☛ Demand as a blurbster of other would-be best-sellers.

A Word of Caution!

The Thomas Success Factors Grid is not as easy to use as it looks.

Some first-time The Thomas Grid users, for example, have inadvertently placed the Success Factors in the wrong position on the axes, thus leading to an incorrect upper right Quadrant combination. This can lead to disastrous consequences, especially when The Thomas Grid is distributed throughout a large organization.

Just one example will suffice to demonstrate the dangers of a poorly configured The Thomas Grid:

Business Success Factors • INCORRECT!

	Good	Slow
Fast	Fast & Good	**Fast & Slow!**
Bad	Bad & Good	Bad & Slow

This is an actual The Thomas Grid that was circulated to several thousand employees of a Fortune 100 company. Within a few short weeks, the entire company was in chaos as everyone in the organization attempted valiantly — but, alas, in vain — to work Fast & Slow at the same time.

It seems that senior management — rather than retain an outside consultant to develop their The Thomas Grid — had attempted to do it themselves. Desperate, and unable to determine the cause of their problems, they called me in. Fortunately, I was able to pinpoint the difficulty within just a few days.

Now, I am pleased to say that the company is back on the Fast & Good track where they belong.

Call 1-888-4-STHOMAS for
The Smeaton-Thomas Success
Factors Grid® Kit.

The Pyramid Paradigm of Organizational Structure

One of the most important roles for any Leader is to determine the optimal organizational structure, one that supports the Leader's vision and best suits his or her management style.

The most durable and popular organizational paradigm, of course, is the traditional top-down or "pyramid" hierarchy. The pyramid hierarchy dates back to King Khufu, the legendary Egyptian Pharaoh (2590–2567 B.C.).

It looked like this:

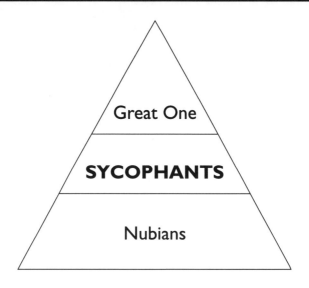

Pyramid Paradigm • 2560 B.C.

Great One

SYCOPHANTS

Nubians

As we can see from the diagram, Khufu ruled from the top, with absolute and final authority over all his "employees." Much to the envy of many present-day Leaders, his portfolio of management methods included execution.

Khufu was also an innovator when it came to systems for compensation and reward. In fact, the highest honor an employee could receive was the guarantee of eternal entombment along with Pharaoh inside the pyramid. Accordingly, punishment and reward looked remarkably similar.

Over the centuries, of course, Khufu's original paradigm has evolved into a structure far more sophisticated and effective — yet strikingly similar to the original. By the mid-20th century, the model had begun to look more like this:

Pyramid Paradigm • Mid-20TH Century

Leader

CONSULTANTS

Greatest Asset (People)

Now, the paradigm is shifting once again. Although the organizational Leader still retains his or her position at the top of the pyramid, it is often as little more than a figurehead. The real power can be found "behind the throne," in the hands of a new class of advisers and experts who supply the Leader with his or her ideas and strategies.

Here's how the classic Pyramid Paradigm looks in more and more organizations worldwide:

Pyramid Paradigm • Emerging

MANAGEMENT CONSULTANTS
(Call 1-888-4-STHOMAS.)

Leader

Teams

Temps

Training "Experts"

Former Employees on Long-Term Contract

Conversation with The Great One

Many of today's Leaders are turning to the great military, spiritual, and political Leaders of the past for advice and counsel, including Attila the Hun, Machiavelli, Sun-Tzu, and even Jesus Christ.

But the wit and wisdom of King Khufu have yet to be incorporated into modern Leadership thought. So, let's use a technique we call "creative visioning" to return to ancient Egypt and take a meeting with King Khufu in his comfortable palace/home office.

SMPT: Greetings, O Great One!

KHUFU: What brings you to Memphis, O He of the Four First Names?

SMPT: I wish to Learn your secret of Leadership, O Great One.

KHUFU: I've had it carved into the wall of my bedchamber. Take a look:

THE GREAT LEADER IS HE WHO

- Rewards those people He can change.
- Executes those people He cannot.
- Does not let on if He cannot tell the difference.

SMPT: How did you arrive at that Learning, O Mighty One? Have you synthesized it from your own managerial experiences, or is it the received wisdom of the ages?

KHUFU: Neither. It comes from Zefti. He's our outside consultant on Fear, Fright, and Intimidation Strategies.

Early consultant Zefti (right) advises King Khufu (left) on Fear, Fright, and Intimidation Strategies.

SMPT: You run a big organization. How do ensure that all your people are operating at the optimal level of fearfulness?

KHUFU: Well, we implemented a major communications program. We kicked it off with a companywide intimidation session that featured a surprise execution. We followed up with small group discussion sessions, supported by a video, cuneiform workbooks, and ritual torturings.

SMPT: Did you synthesize any learning about effective communication for Leaders?

KHUFU: Yes, I've had that one carved into the ceiling of my temple:

TO COMMUNICATE EFFECTIVELY, THE GREAT LEADER SHOULD

- Speak of that which He intends to speak.
- Speak of that which He has said He shall be speaking.
- Speak once more of what He spoke.

SMPT: Great One, if you could send a message to your counterparts, the Leaders of the 21st century, what would you tell them?

KHUFU: I would tell them to take time out to smell the lotuses. When I get ready to enter the Great Pyramid for the last time, I doubt I'll be saying, "I wish I'd spent more time at the Palace!"

Call 1-888-4-STHOMAS.
MBAs Standing By.

*T*eamwork Exercises for Leaders

Although the Leader generally relies on counsel from colleagues and trusted advisers (call 1-888-4-STHOMAS), as well as tools such as The Thomas Success Factors Grid, he/she alone must make the truly tough decisions and bear responsibility for them.

Given that the tasks of Leadership are essentially individual ones, it may be understandable that Leaders lack highly developed teamworking skills. Take a look at the results of a recent study on the incidence of teamwork among selected professionals:

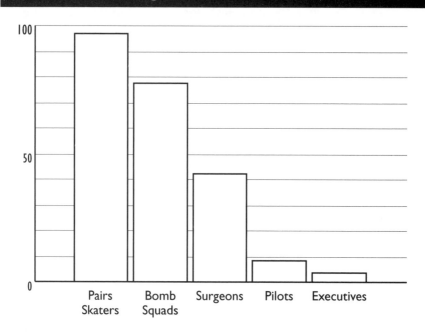

Teamworking Behavior • Selected Professionals

Not surprisingly, Olympic figure skating pairs scored high, whereas business executives scored dismally low — only 3 percent of those senior business executives polled showed even the slightest proclivity toward teamwork. Accordingly, many organizations that have successfully developed a teamworking culture among middle managers and factory personnel are now focusing their teambuilding efforts on senior management.

Of course, the typical team exercises — such as platform jumping, trust falling, obstacle-course racing, and rope swinging — are often not relevant to the complex needs of Leadership teams.

That's why a whole new breed of exercise has begun to appear in educational programs and Leadership seminars around the world. These intriguing new initiatives seek to parallel the complexity and urgency that the typical Leadership team (such as an operating committee or a board of directors) might face.

Bomb Squad

This exercise begins with an anonymous telephone call from a member of a terrorist group (role-played by the Facilitator), informing the Team that a powerful bomb has been placed in a public area — preferably in a building owned by the Team's company — and that it has been set to explode within 17 minutes.

The Team members must work together to suit up in protective clothing, proceed to the location, find the bomb, and remove it from the area before it explodes. For maximum Learning, a real bomb should be used.

If the Team fails to neutralize the bomb, the exercise is considered a failure and — if anyone remains alive — they must repeat it.

Note the high level of collaborative behavior displayed by participants in the Bomb Squad Exercise.

Roll the New Product Marshmallow across the Hot Coals of Development

This exercise is designed to help Leaders who have little or no experience in new product creation to better understand the issues encountered by development teams.

Here's how it works:

1. Divide the participating Leaders into two Teams.

2. Provide each Team with a marshmallow.

3. Instruct the executives to push the marshmallow, using their nose only, across a white-hot bed of fiery coals. (Marshmallow = product prototype. Coals = development process.)

4. The winning Team is the one that gets the marshmallow to the far side of the coals without incinerating either the marshmallow or themselves. (Far side of coals = market.)

To make the exercise even more challenging, the Team members should be stripped naked, blindfolded, and lashed together with a high-speed, fire-resistant T-3 data cable.

The Big Ship

In this extremely popular exercise, Leaders take charge of a large ship, such as an ocean liner or a retired aircraft carrier.

The Leadership Team must maneuver the ship (representing the company) from Point A to Point B, while encountering a variety of events that simulate changes in business conditions; for example:

☞ **Negative Profitability.** The Team suddenly discovers that the ship is headed directly for a reef. They must work together to "turn the big ship around" before it plows into the coral and sinks.

☞ **Brain Drain.** Key crew members receive attractive employment offers from competing Captains and begin abandoning ship. The Team must determine whether to improve working conditions and increase compensation or risk a potentially violent, full-scale mutiny.

Note: The Big Ship exercise, although popular, is not inexpensive. It requires the chartering of an ocean liner, loading in several thousand gallons of diesel fuel, purchasing fancy-dress uniforms, etc. The most cost-effective solution is to work with a qualified consultancy experienced in Big Ship Team Training. Call 1-888-4-STHOMAS.

Diner

In this exercise, Leaders work as the staff of an operating road-side diner. The exercise begins by assigning each Leader a job, such as fry-cook, prep chef, counterperson, dishwasher, or cashier. The Leaders then receive training in relevant skills, responsibilities, and behaviors, if any are required.

They then spend three days operating the diner. The exercise can be adapted to simulate any number of business situations; for example:

☛ **Hostile Takeover.** A crazed gunman (usually the Facilitator) bursts into the diner, threatens to shoot the manager, takes the cashier hostage, and demands that the fry-cook prepare a grilled cheese sandwich "just the way I like it" without establishing any specific measurement criteria (e.g., crustiness, cheese meltness). This exercise is also ideal for a discussion of Dealing with the Difficult Customer.

☛ **Crisis Management.** A customer becomes violently ill after eating an order of unrefrigerated salmon salad. She threatens to initiate legal action and organize a customer boycott. Leaders must work as a Team to decide whether to handle the situation as a public relations issue or as a medical emergency.

☛ **Change Management.** Once the Leaders begin to function competently as a Team, the manager (role-played, often with relish, by the Facilitator) introduces a number of unsettling workplace changes without warning, training, or explanation of long-range strategy.

The changes might involve implementing new technologies, such as a digital Fryolator or computerized short-order entry system. They might involve new processes, such as an improved method of Counter Washdown. Or they might involve new performance measures, such as Total Elapsed Time from Order Being Shouted to Platter Delivery.

Changing a Tire while Traveling at 80 Miles per Hour
This is a highly effective and inexpensive alternative to the Big Ship exercise. In it, Leaders work together to change a rapidly deflating tire on a rental automobile while traveling along a section of abandoned highway.

The car must maintain a speed of 80 miles per hour and the tire must be changed before it completely deflates. The exercise must be completed without any Team members being injured and without the car crashing into any obstructions. Many Leaders report that the experience is almost identical to their normal daily routines.

Choose *Your* Success Model!

Those who populate the pantheon of Leaders change as the times change. In the '70s, for example, many businesspeople looked to World War II military leaders — such as George S. Patton — for inspiration. Interestingly enough, military leaders are back in the limelight in the late 1990s.

General Colin Powell sharpened his Leadership skills with The Thomas Big Ship Teamwork Exercise.

In the '80s, sports personalities rose to prominence as Leadership models.

Golf great
Arnold Palmer
was a popular
Leadership model
in the 1980s but,
because of the
nonteamworking
nature of golf,
fell out of favor
in the '90s.

In the early '90s, we looked to new sources for Leadership wisdom, including great historical personalities (Attila the Hun), television heroes (Mr. Spock from *Star Trek*), and even cartoon characters (Piglet).

☞ **EXERCISE.** Select a well-known Leadership model for yourself and your organization — one who has not been used or written about. Learn as much as you can about him or her. Dress up in clothes that the Leader might wear. Try running your organization the way that Leader might have run his or hers.

Just to get you started, here are a few candidates whose highly successful Leadership styles have yet to be applied to the world of traditional business:

Don King.
Action-oriented,
numbers-driven.
Achieves results
through others.

Karl Marx.
Thought leader,
good with concepts.

Madonna.
High-profile,
outspoken.
Leads by example.

THE SECOND LEARNING

COMMUNICATION IS IMPORTANT

"Few people will pay attention when you speak.

They will forget most of what you said.

They will remember forever your tiniest error.

In short, effective communication is impossible."

STEPHEN MICHAEL PETER THOMAS

*C*reating a Humor-Free Workplace

To communicate a business vision throughout the organization, the Leader may employ a variety of rhetorical techniques, including anecdote, metaphor, song, exhortation, even prayer. Humor, however, is out.

Why? Because humor generally involves "making fun" of such fundamental human characteristics as cultural origin, gender, or physical traits. Consider, for example, the most popular categories of workplace jokes over the past two decades:

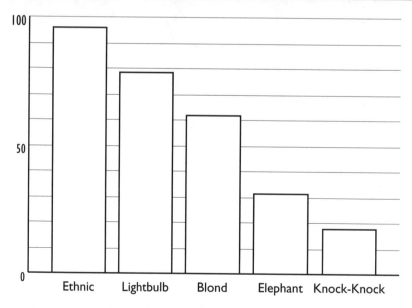

Most Popular Joke Types • 1975–1995

(Source: American Institute for Jocularity Research)

Each of these joke types creates humor by denigrating the intellectual, cultural, or physical traits of a particular subgroup of the population. This is completely unacceptable in today's society.

Accordingly, many progressive organizations have sought to create "humor-free" workplace environments. They recognize, however, that this cannot happen overnight and have developed a number of ways to help people transition away from the laughter habit.

The first step, of course, is to create a change in attitude — to help people understand that jokes can be a primary source of divisiveness and cultural pain. Workers are encouraged to *present* a joke rather than actually *tell* it. To present a joke is similar to telling a joke, except that all elements of performance and emotional involvement have been removed.

Here you can see the difference:

Telling a Joke

Presenting a Joke

While the joke is being presented, the listeners are encouraged to take note of aspects of the communication that they might previously have found funny, such as amusing sounds, punchlines, or sight gags. Then, once the presentation has been completed, the presenter and listeners are encouraged to discuss the joke. Ideally, this will involve an exploration of the assumptions and biases that underlie it and the sources of its so-called humor.

In practice, the presentation and discussion of a joke looks and sounds quite similar to the actual telling of one. But, in reality, both presenter and listeners are simply working together to help eradicate inappropriate workplace humor.

Some Human Resource departments have developed sophisticated tools to help with the effort. Perhaps the most successful of these is The Risibility Index. It enables the HR professional to analyze the offensive content of a joke and then calculate its numerical Risibility Index Rating. Here, for example, is the analysis of a joke about a sexual situation involving a vacuum cleaner salesperson and a member of management who affects an alternative lifestyle:

Risibility Index • Vacuum Cleaner Salesperson Joke

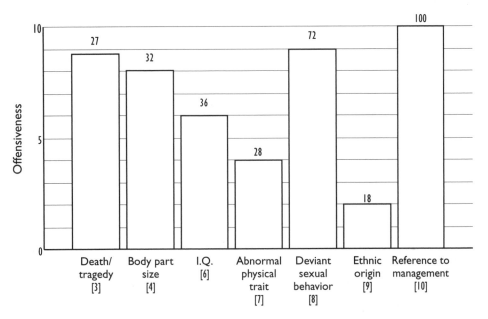

Content Type [Weighting]

The joke received a Risibility Index Rating of 268. Now contrast that rating with the Risibility Index Rating for that most innocuous of traditional jokes:

Risibility Index • Chicken Crosses Road Joke

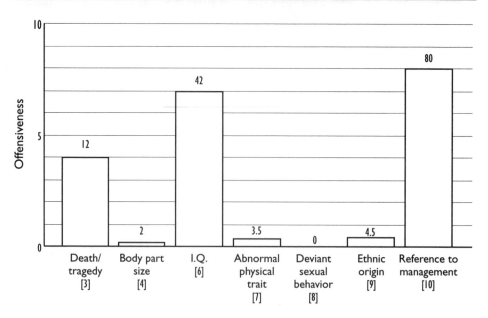

The chicken joke received a Rating of 144.

HR professionals can use the Risibility Index to establish a corporate standard for acceptable humor, by using a benchmark joke — such as the chicken joke. The corporate spec may vary from organization to organization based upon a number of variables. Here are the average Risibility Index Ratings accepted in selected workplaces:

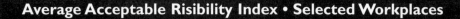

Average Acceptable Risibility Index • Selected Workplaces

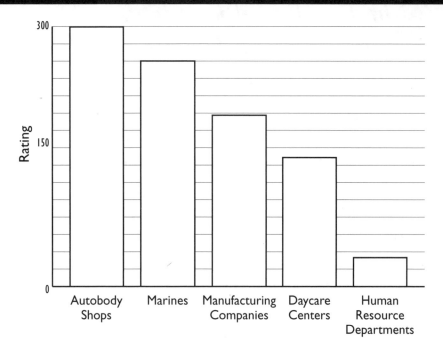

The Risibility Index has proven highly effective in reducing the incidence and offensiveness of workplace humor. In fact, many HR professionals report a tremendous increase in telephone-call volume to their offices from people wishing to present the latest jokes or to inquire about the Risibility Index Rating of jokes already in circulation.

In one company I know, the Risibility call volume has become so great that it has established a Risibility Intranet site on which you can hear all the latest jokes presented. Or, you can enter your own "joke," and the Risibility server will calculate its Risibility Index Rating.

It all may seem very similar to traditional workplace humor, with one exception — it's not actually "funny."

*T*he Illustrated Guide to Global Hand Gestures and Facial Expressions

As more and more companies conduct business globally, the need for communicating in a foreign language has risen concomitantly. However, only a small percentage of businesspeople — especially those in the United States — have any facility with a second language. Although many companies provide language training, we have found that it is rarely successful.

Take heart! More and more businesspeople are communicating effectively through a combination of internationally recognized words, phrases, gestures, and facial expressions. This extremely subtle, highly sophisticated Global Communication Method can be used for even the most complex or technical conversations.

Although it can take a significant time commitment to completely master the Global Communication Method (often as long as 45 minutes), it is possible to grasp a few of the basics within seconds.

We begin with the two basic communication Attitudes:

☞ **The *I Love to Listen* Attitude.** This indicates that you are mentally prepared to communicate and employ your active listening skills.

"I Love to Listen!"

Remember, active listening skills include:

• Adopting an earnest look, as if you actually care about what the other person has to say.

• Nodding from time to time, to indicate that you are paying attention and have not dozed off.

• Making small vocalizations, such as "Mmm" or "Ah-ha," to keep your tongue, larynx, and soft palate flexible and lubricated so as to be ready when it's your turn to talk.

☛ **The *Can I Talk Now?* Attitude.** This indicates that you have something to say and alerts the intended Listener to assume the *I Love to Listen* Attitude.

"Can I Talk Now?"

Now, here are a few common phrases that come up often in international business, translated into the appropriate Global Communication Method facial expression/hand gesture:

"Hello!"

"How is business?"

"I am experiencing a virtually
unignorable biological emergency."

"I will ignore the nationality-biased
remark you just made."

Okay, I imagine that your reaction to these basics is, "Hey, I know the Global Communication Method already!" That's fine — as far as it goes. But let's take a look at a business conversation that's a bit more complex:

VISITOR: I have traveled 7,000 miles to inspect your newly installed Hutt Special 48-up, multimaterial, variable-pitch, computer-aided molding system.

HOST: Unfortunately, we experienced a malfunction of the control software that caused the system to run wildly out of control, catch fire, and explode.

VISITOR: Never mind. Instead, why don't I sit in on the training session you have scheduled on the subject of The Role of Risk Management in Reducing the Incidence and Severity of Lost-Time, Swing Shift Safety Recordables.

"Never mind."

HOST: Unfortunately, that session was canceled because the employees are all on strike this morning and this afternoon is the company picnic.

VISITOR: Never mind. By the way, did I mention that you need to cut operating costs by 12 percent, reduce headcount by 62 percent, improve productivity by 197 percent, and boost your ROI to 32 percent by early next week or we'll close your facility?

HOST: Why don't we have some lunch and discuss it further. We have prepared a special meal for you of elk broth, grilled eel sausage, and deep-fried periwinkles from the River Bluge.

"Grilled eel?"

VISITOR: Isn't that what you served Pat Smith last time he was over?

HOST: Yes, he told us how much he enjoyed it, just before he died.

See, it's simple! Now you try it!

ℰ ublic Speaking in Our Non-Linear Age

For years — centuries perhaps — public speakers and their speech writers have relied on a simple, highly effective formula for structuring their presentations and other communications:

The Tell 'Em Communication Structure

1.
Tell 'Em
What You're
Gonna Tell 'Em

2.
Tell 'Em

3.
Tell 'Em
What You
Told 'Em

I'm here to tell you that the formula no longer works for many audiences, especially younger ones. That's because their communication styles have been shaped by the media. Thus they prefer:

☞ **Non-Linearity**. Communication no longer flows in a unidirectional, linear fashion. Audiences prefer a random structure similar to what they get when channel surfing on 300-channel cable TV.

☛ **Interactivity.** The speaker who stands rigidly behind a podium, delivers a lecture, and expects the audience to remain passive will fail. Today's audience wishes to participate in the communication. (Just as you can in this book!)

☛ **Reduced Attention Span.** Over the past two decades, the attention span of the average businessperson has fallen drastically, as evidenced by the amount of time people were willing to devote to these communications vehicles:

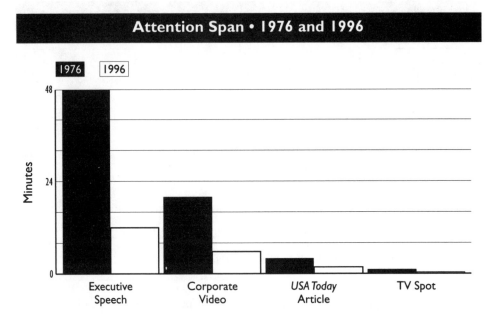

☛ **Data, Interesting Info, Market Research, and Factoids.** People cannot understand abstract ideas until those ideas are made concrete with the latest Department of Agriculture data or the results of a Gartner Group study. The data need not necessarily directly support the message or make any particular point whatsoever.

Accordingly, public speakers are adjusting their styles to our non-linear communication age. The following popular formula is simply a slight refinement of the old:

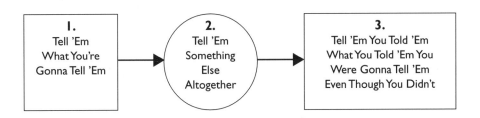

The Modified Tell 'Em Communication Structure

1.	**2.**	**3.**
Tell 'Em What You're Gonna Tell 'Em	Tell 'Em Something Else Altogether	Tell 'Em You Told 'Em What You Told 'Em You Were Gonna Tell 'Em Even Though You Didn't

This structure is most appealing for the speaker because it frees him or her of the need to prepare the presentation or to deliver ideas in any logical sequence. However, research shows that this method tends to slightly reduce message retention on the part of the audience. For most executive presentations, however, there are so few messages to comprehend that it doesn't really matter.

The most powerful public speakers of today have adopted a wholly new, completely random presentation style that looks something like this:

Non-Linear Communication Structure • New Paradigm

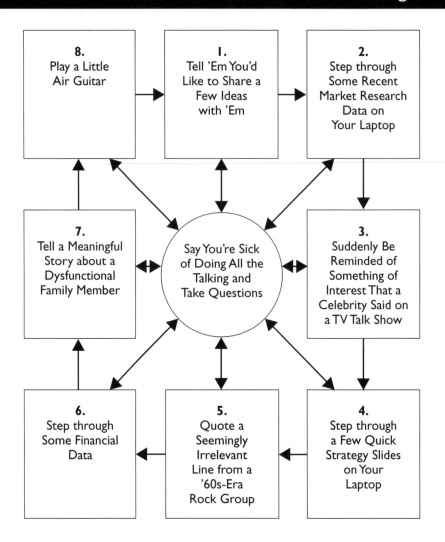

8.
Play a Little
Air Guitar

1.
Tell 'Em You'd
Like to Share a
Few Ideas
with 'Em

2.
Step through
Some Recent
Market Research
Data on
Your Laptop

7.
Tell a Meaningful
Story about a
Dysfunctional
Family Member

Say You're Sick
of Doing All the
Talking and
Take Questions

3.
Suddenly Be
Reminded of
Something of
Interest That a
Celebrity Said on
a TV Talk Show

6.
Step through
Some Financial
Data

5.
Quote a
Seemingly
Irrelevant
Line from a
'60s-Era
Rock Group

4.
Step through
a Few Quick
Strategy Slides
on Your
Laptop

By restructuring their presentations using the New Paradigm, communicators are able to increase audience enjoyment while reducing audience anxiety about whether they can retain enough of what they're hearing to answer questions about it later. Research shows that such speeches are 96 percent more likely to lead to positive outcomes than traditionally structured speeches are.

The real power of this structure is that the components can be used in any order — the numbers in the diagram suggest just one possible flow. It makes absolutely no difference to the effectiveness or meaning of the presentation if you:

☛ Start with air guitar and end with strategy.

☛ Start with questions and end with financial data.

☛ Start with a meaningful story and end with the same story.

Whatever!

TIME OUT! Try *Your* Communication Skills!

Below you will find photographs of a number of well-known communicators, captured in the midst of an important communication and employing one or more of the Global Hand Gestures and Facial Expressions.

The key elements of the gesture and/or expression are identified. Your assignment is to analyze the meaning of each element and determine what the speaker might be communicating! (Answers on p. 63.)

Good luck!

I) JESSE JACKSON

b.
Head at angle.

a.
Clenched teeth.

c.
Arm extended,
palm up.

2) AL GORE

a.
U-shaped
smile.

b.
Guru nearby.

c.
Extended
forefinger.

3) BORIS YELTSIN

b.
Arched
eyebrows.

c.
Snarly
upper lip.

a.
Bent pinky.

ANSWERS

1) JESSE JACKSON

a. *"Leadership is hard."*

b. *"I am human."*

c. *"What can you do?"*

2) AL GORE

a. *"I am delightful."*

b. *"Communication is important."*

c. *"I am smart."*

3) BORIS YELTSIN

a. *"I am lying."*

b. *"Do you have a problem with that?"*

c. *"Change is different."*

THE THIRD LEARNING

CHANGE IS DIFFERENT

"The only constant is that people keep talking about change without actually changing."

STEPHEN MICHAEL PETER THOMAS

*R*esisting Change: *The Forgetting Organization*

In an attempt to better manage change, many companies have sought to become Learning Organizations — in which continuous learning, growth, and change become a way of life. It's a powerful idea in theory, but many organizations have been stymied in their attempts. Not only do they stubbornly refuse to Learn, many of them seem to be forgetting what they already know.

Why?

Careful observation of many such "Forgetting Organizations" reveals the most common causes:

☛ **Mental Overload.** Today, the amount of information and knowledge that swirls through an organization is so overwhelming that most employees feel lucky to remember what they Learned 10 minutes ago or where they parked their car — let alone the great corporate Learnings of the decades.

☛ **Skeleton in Closet.** Most organizations harbor at least one collective memory so deep and dismal that no one dares speak of it aloud. It is often easier for these people to simply forget everything that happened in the past, rather than risk mentioning something that might somehow invoke the terrible thing. Typical skeletons include:

• *Product Disaster.* At Polaroid, for example, you should avoid the question, "Hey, did you guys ever think about making instant movie film?" Similarly, it's not wise to ask a FedEx person whatever happened to that ZapMail idea. You may not want to talk to Bankers Trust about complex hedging instruments.

• *Trouble with the Founder.* If the Founder is no longer on the premises but is not very old or (preferably) dead, there might be a problem worth forgetting. He/she might have been ousted (Ken Olsen, Steve Jobs). He/she might have been arrested (Stew Leonard, Michael Milken). Or he/she may have crossed over into megalomania or some other form of lunacy (Ross Perot).

☞ **No Witnesses.** People Learn best from each other. But in down-sized organizations, virtual organizations, or organizations with high turnover, there may not be anyone who has been on staff long enough to teach anything.

This tendency to want to forget can severely hinder a company's ability to grow, change, and Learn. How can these Forgetters change to become Learners? One effective method is to reconnect with their cultural roots, to rediscover (or invent, if necessary) their corporate personality. The best place to start is with the Founding Environment — yes, the physical birth-place of the organization. Often the nature of the Founding Environment provides powerful clues to the essential nature of the organization.

Let's look at the most popular Founding Environments of just one type of organization, the technology company, over the past 50 years:

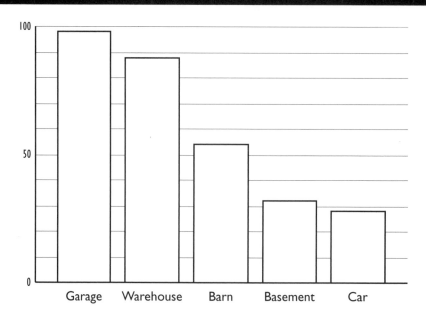

Popular Founding Environments • Technology Companies

Let's examine the most popular Founding Environment — the garage — more closely. Why do Founders, especially of technology companies, so often favor the garage as their first headquarters? When asked, they usually cite such practical considerations as low cost and convenience. However, deeper probing often reveals far more complex and intriguing pyscho-emotional reasons for the choice.

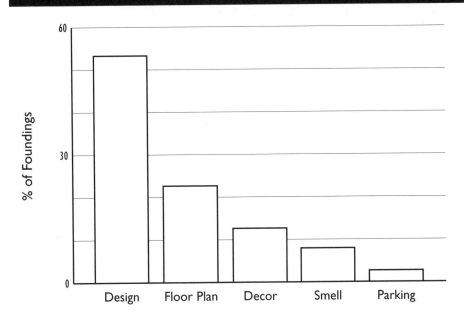

Reasons for Founding Company in Garage

By comparing the Founding Environment with the current environment of the most and least successful companies, we come to the following conclusion:

Successful technology companies operate in environments with characteristics similar to those of the Founding Environment. Conversely, the unsuccessful companies have "forgotten" their roots.

Founding environment of a leading technology company.

Look at the sprawling complexes of the great garage-founded technology companies (e.g., Hewlett-Packard and Digital Equipment), and you will find them toiling away in environments that look and feel very much like garages:

- *Design.* Long, flat-roofed, extremely dull-looking buildings.

- *Floor Plan.* Big open spaces with cubicled offices reminiscent of garage bays, only smaller.

- *Decor.* Chosen for durability rather than aesthetic concerns. Artwork that looks as if it was created by family members of founders.

• *Smell.* A pervasive — oddly appealing — aroma that mingles the distinctive scents of cement, insulation, lubricant, fireproofing, and hot machines.

• *Parking.* A heavy emphasis on accommodation for the motor vehicle.

The Learning? You can take the company out of the garage, but you can't take the garage out of the company.

Companies that have relocated in locations that do not have the characteristics of the Founding Environment can quickly reconnect with their roots through regular application of Founding Environment Scent, available in a variety of aromas, including Garage and Barn.

Call 1-888-4-STHOMAS.

 orgetting: Leading Indicators

Organizational Forgetting may creep up on a company so gradually that it does not realize it is Forgetting until it is so far gone that it Forgets what it's like to remember anything. A company that is beginning to Forget will exhibit a variety of odd behaviors, including:

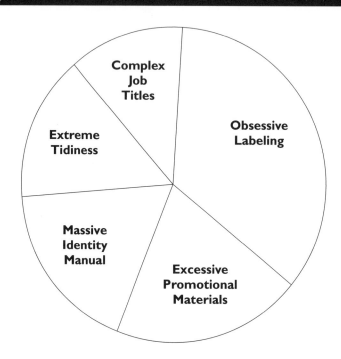

It is as if people within these companies sense they are losing touch with their cultural roots and are desperately attempting to hold on to what memories they can.

These are the Leading Indicators of Forgetting, and they generally emerge in the following sad stages of decline:

☞ **Phase 1: Complex Job Titles.** As the company gradually Forgets what it is doing and why it is in existence, the first step is to define individual responsibilities more precisely and with greater detail. Thus, simple and descriptive titles become so detailed and abstruse that, in a sad irony, they become virtually impossible to remember (e.g., Corporate Officer for the Acquisition of Retention of Knowledge).

☞ **Phase 2: Massive Identity Manual.** The company develops a massive series of guidelines that dictate how the corporate logo, colors, typeface, etc., should be applied to every form, object, medium, and scrap of tangible substance.

☞ **Phase 3: Excessive Promotional Materials.** Every department, discipline, work group, facility, task force, and project team suddenly gets the urge to create a brochure, newsletter, presentation, video, or Web site that documents in excruciating detail what they are doing and why.

☞ **Phase 4: Obsessive Labeling.** This is perhaps the most pathetic manifestation of Forgetting. People are overcome with a desire to affix permanent labels to every object in the company that has even the slightest need to be explained or clarified.

Here, for example, are the signs I observed in just one kitchen in an organization that had reached an advanced stage of Forgetting:

• Employee Food Service Location #37-East.

• Do Not Store Anything in This Cabinet.

• Electrical Outlet #EOT-965/Kitchen #37-East.

• If Rotten Items Are Found in This Refrigerator, Call Ext. 552 Immediately.

• If You Are Choking to Death, See *Emergency Choking to Death Procedures* Poster Posted in Employee Food Service Location #49-West.

☛ **Phase 5: Extreme Tidiness.** In this final stage of Forgetting, employees have so completely forgotten what they are all about that they have lost the ability to concoct new job titles, to apply the Identity Manual recommendations, or even to label previously unlabeled items.

Instead, in order to keep reasonably active, they spend their days ensuring that the corporate grass is mowed; that bark mulch is applied to all shrubbery; that the reception areas are free of all dust, lint, or discarded coffee cups; and that bathrooms are well stocked with paper towels, toilet paper, and liquid soap.

The Learning: Cleanliness is next to Chapter 11.

An Unexpected Consequence of Change

Today, the most rapidly changing aspect of the workplace is, of course, technology. We have found that even as a technology innovation solves a specific business problem, it often creates new and unexpected changes.

For example, the precipitous rise in the use of one common communications technology has provoked a crisis in another area of business activity: new product development. I can sketch its dimensions for you by asking a few simple questions:

Q: Do you believe that we operate in a fast-paced, fiercely competitive, global business environment in which new players might emerge at any moment from any location?

A: 1. No, we do not conduct our business on this planet.
2. Yes.

Q: Do you believe that, to remain competitive, companies must offer a steady stream of new products with meaningful, customer-discernible, value-adding features?

A: 1. No, we can get along with low-quality products we first introduced back in the sixties.
2. Yes.

Q: To develop innovative, breakthrough products that meet customer demands, that are manufacturable, safe, and environmentally friendly, and that can deliver a return on development costs within two to three weeks, which is the enabling technology that your designers rely on most?

A: 1. Clusters of high-performance CAD workstations.
2. Backs of envelopes.

Q: With the proliferation of high-speed, platform-independent, wide-bandwidth, graphically rich communications networks, which of the following communications channels do you use the most often?

A: 1. The U.S. Postal Service.
2. E-mail.

Are you beginning to see the crisis?

Because the use of E-mail is on the rise...
the supply of envelopes is waning.
Because envelopes are a key product development technology...
our competitiveness is in grave peril!

Just one chart makes the dimensions of the crisis painfully clear:

Relation of E-Mail Messages to New Product Innovation • 1990–1995

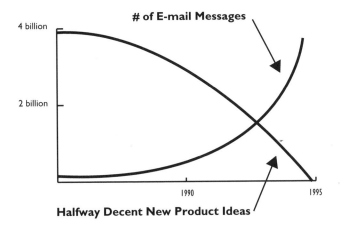

This is most alarming when you consider that the great majority of the world's most important product innovations and technological breakthroughs have begun life on the back of an envelope. Here are just a few examples:

Envelope-Based New Product Sketch • The Wheel

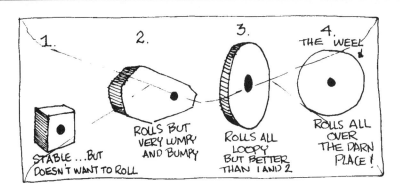

Envelope-Based New Product Sketch • The Sandwich

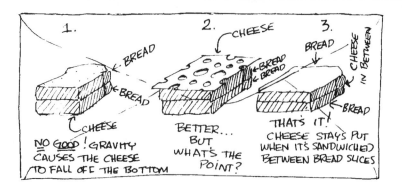

Fortunately, the picture actually might not be quite as bleak as the data make it appear. New product people in progressive companies are finding ways around the Envelope Problem by turning to other sources of scrap paper: cocktail napkins, airline boarding passes, and, in a supreme irony, the backs of E-mail printouts.

Call 1-888-4-STHOMAS to purchase your Development Kit with blank envelopes in bulk. These high-quality paper envelopes without return addresses, and with special flat-glued seams, facilitate sketching.

Call 1-888-4-STHOMAS.

*B*ringing Change Back Home: *Meet the Glinster Family!*

In recent years, as the pace of business has intensified, more and more time-pressed managers and Leaders have sought new and more effective methods of changing and improving their organizational performance. They have mastered a variety of disciplines that have enabled them to do everything from optimize their physical/mental peak performance zones to better manage their time.

Many of these managers — even those operating at 97 to 98 percent workplace efficiency — relentlessly seek new areas in which to further sharpen their competitive edge. And you know where they're finding plenty of room for change and improvement? Not in the workplace, but in the domestic environment. Yes, at home.

Think about it. Even if you spend 10 to 12 hours on the job each day, that still leaves 50 percent of your time — or more — that could be optimized. And I think most of us would have to admit that we tolerate a great deal more waste and process redundancy in our domestic lives than we would in the office or on the shop floor.

Ask yourself the following questions:

Q: If my after-hours me applied for a job to my workplace me, would I hire me?

Q: If I applied my domestic achievement standards to my workplace tasks, would I have accomplished anything at all today?

Q: If I were to benchmark my domestic processes against best of breed, would mine be considered a "world-class household"?

These are the very questions that Loretta Glinster asked herself — and she didn't like the answers she heard. Loretta is a senior executive with a multi-national maker of lo-fat salty snacks. Husband Al is creative director in the New Media department of a large advertising agency. The Glinsters have seven great kids, ranging from three months to 32 years old.

Needless to say, time is at a premium in the Glinster household. And even with two healthy incomes, money is always an issue when you have several kids in exclusive private schools and must take two family vacations each year, at least one of which is outside the continental United States.

It so happened that Loretta's salty snack company had recently reengineered their core processes, which resulted in significant gains in productivity, new product innovation, and customer satisfaction. Loretta decided to organize her family and set about some serious Domestic Process Reengineering (DPR).

First, the Glinsters analyzed their key family processes to determine which ones consumed the most hours per week. Here's what they found:

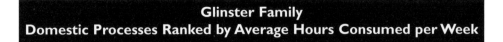

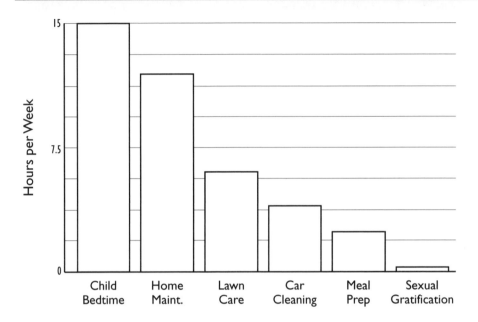

Yes, the Glinster family Bedtime Domestic Process was the number one time consumer, at nearly 15 hours per week. Home Maintenance, Lawn Care, and Car Cleaning ranked second, third, and fourth, with negligible amounts of time devoted to the Meal Preparation and Sexual Gratification Processes.

Obviously, if the Glinsters were looking for breakthrough change, they would have to tackle the Bedtime Process. But first, they decided to hone their reengineering skills by attempting a pilot project. After much discussion, they settled on Meal Preparation.

By designing menus with no more than two dishes and eliminating recipes that called for chopping or mincing, they managed to reduce Meal Prep time by nearly 38 percent — a gain of nearly an hour and a half per person per week.

Heartened, the Glinsters knocked off a number of Home Maintenance, Lawn Care, and Car Cleaning redesign projects, which netted them another 4.8 hours. Loretta and Al even found a way to reduce the number of steps involved in their already quite efficient Sexual Gratification Process, thus shaving nearly seven minutes off Time-to-Gratification.

Then, having flexed their muscles with this "low-hanging fruit" of Domestic Process Redesign, they were ready for the Big One. The first step for the brave Glinsters was to analyze the Bedtime Process in its current state. They found that the typical Bedtime routine required 21 steps and consumed a total of 37 minutes per child! Take a look...

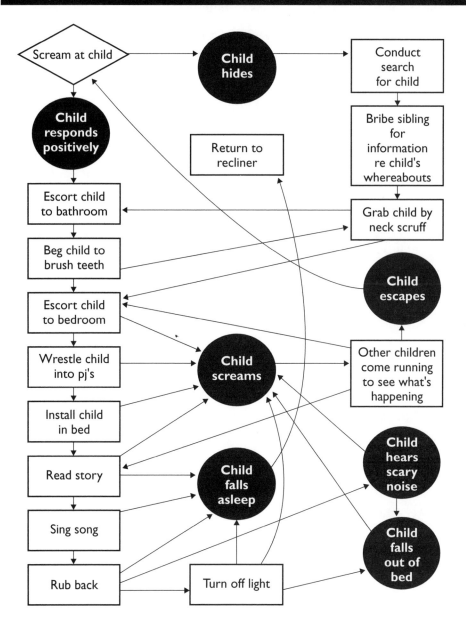

Glinster Family Bedtime Process • Before Redesign

Needless to say, all Glinster family members were amazed at this finding and enthusiastically sought ways to redesign the process. They were able to achieve incremental improvements with such changes as reading shorter books, humming rather than singing, and starting the bribing procedure earlier in the process. However, they finally realized that only radical redesign would yield breakthrough improvement. And that's how they mustered the courage — for that is what it was — *to eliminate every step in the process that did not directly contribute to achieving the Goal: Child Falls Asleep.* Here's how the process looked after the Glinsters had bitten the bullet:

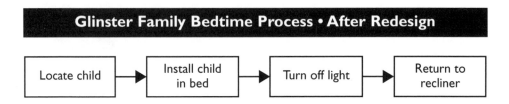

Glinster Family Bedtime Process • After Redesign

| Locate child | Install child in bed | Turn off light | Return to recliner |

Okay, the process might make some parents uncomfortable. You might say, "Well, what about tooth decay? What about family bonding? Won't the kid need to get up in the middle of the night to go to the bathroom?"

Well, you have to break some eggs to make an omelet. The point is that the Glinsters, unlike 99 percent of American families, can now get one child into bed in three minutes and all seven of them tucked in (including the 32-year-old) within 20 minutes. That's a productivity improvement of some 900 percent!

I think you would have to agree that the gains outweigh the losses — and that we'll be seeing a lot more DPR in progressive suburbs worldwide.

THE FOURTH LEARNING

PEOPLE
ARE HUMAN

"Tardiness.

Lust.

Funny moods.

Golf.

Smart companies are working to better manage
the vagaries of human behavior."

STEPHEN MICHAEL PETER THOMAS

The Hidden Cost of Not Starting on Time

Even the most disciplined businesspeople — even those of us with brilliant vision, clearly stated Success Factors, superbly reengineered processes, consistent Learning habits, and advanced teamworking skills — still exhibit behaviors that are maddeningly irrational and inconsistent with our business goals. In a word, we are human. The most common of these human behaviors, of course, is the inability to manage time wisely or well.

Consider the most basic Time Management problem: starting on time. Study after study has shown that On-Time Start Performance is so poor that it threatens to cripple the global economy.

Here's proof:

☞ In 1996, only 3 percent of planned events actually started on time. That's down from 6 percent On-Time Starts in 1951 and 7 percent in 1937.

☞ The later an Event starts, the later it finishes. In fact, each Late Starting Minute translates into seven minutes by the time whatever it is finally wraps up.

☞ The cumulative effect of all these Late Starts is that we, as a planet, are approximately two years behind. Everything that should have been completed in April of 1997 will not actually be done until late 1999.

Let's take a look at the major problem areas:

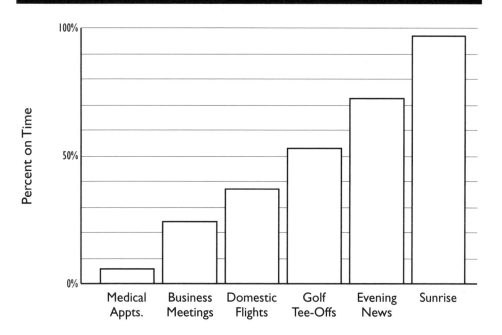

You can see that Business Meetings rank just slightly higher than Medical Appointments in On-Time Start Performance. That's distressing enough. But when you consider the reasons for Business Meeting delay, the picture grows even gloomier.

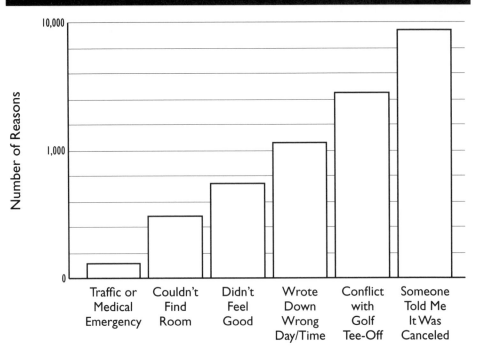

What does this all mean?

If we continue our Late Start behaviors, it may be necessary to insert two more years into this decade, thus delaying the start of the New Millennium. Estimated cost worldwide: $1.7 trillion.

This, clearly, is an untenable situation that must be dealt with immediately.

& nforcement:
The Next Step in Time Management

Yes, we have a time problem. Yes, it's serious.

But, YES! We can solve it. How? By taking the next, desperately need-ed step in Time Management. It's time to add some real teeth to those com-plicated Time Management Systems and Methods that promise to help you organize and prioritize your time, make your work more productive, and align every waking minute with some personal, professional, organizational, or spiritual objective.

All too often, the actual result of these systems is that you're out three days of training, several hundred bucks for an ostrich binder, and 12 pounds of odd-sized paper; and you have a persistent feeling of guilt and inadequacy that you're not spending three hours a day managing your diary.

So what's needed? Good, old-fashioned, politically incorrect Enforcement! A Time Management System that doesn't let you miss an appointment. And if you do, it punishes you.

Only through Enforcement — and Enforcement with real teeth in it — can we ensure that the majority of the employ-ees of the world's organizations will do what they are sup-posed to do, when they are supposed to do it!

Without the application of the Time Management techniques described below, not only do we risk a delay in the start of the New Millennium, we may find it necessary to a call a moratorium on the scheduling of all new business meetings until the time problem is resolved. The thought of doing business without the prospect of planning, scheduling, rescheduling, postponing, or canceling new meetings is virtually insupportable.

Now, before describing the Enforcement System, let's take a moment to review the history of Time Management. Over the years, all kinds of systems have been developed to help businesspeople plan and manage time:

The String-on-Finger Method

The so-called String-on-Finger Method was very popular in the United States — especially in rural manufacturing facilities where many folks were unfamiliar with writing — beginning in the early 1800s.

The Method was easy to Learn and easy to use. The businessperson who wished to remember an important appointment or To-Do item simply lashed a length of common household string around the tip of the forefinger. Once the appointment was over or the To-Do item completed, the person would unwrap the string and set it aside.

Although crude, this Method was highly effective because the reduced flow of blood to the fingertip made it throb or "go dead," making this simple mnemonic device very difficult to ignore.

String-on-Finger Time Management System • Circa 1812

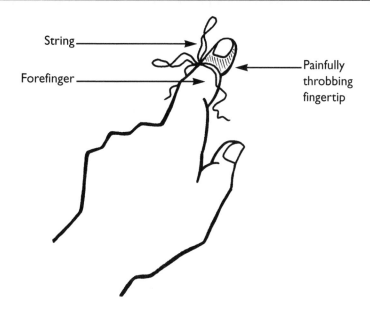

String —————————————→

Forefinger ——————————————→

Painfully
throbbing
fingertip

The String Method was not without limitations. For example, it was nearly impossible to add any specific detail about the To-Do item — such as what it was, when it was, why it was, who it was with, and any other information that might provide the faintest clue as to why this bit of string had been wrapped so tightly and inconveniently around the finger.

In addition, the String Method was short on archiving capability. Although a few well-organized businesspeople might keep their used strings for later review, you just can't tell much by rummaging through a bunch of strings all tangled up in a used cigar box.

String-on-Finger Time Management System • Archiving Method

The To-Do List

A huge advance over String-on-Finger, the To-Do List is believed to have been invented in England around the start of the Industrial Revolution.

The To-Do List, of course, has been so fully assimilated into the workplace that it hardly seems a Time Management Method at all. Yet it was a breakthrough in its day because it was highly portable, employed readily available technologies (paper, writing instrument), was easily learned, and enabled the user to indicate what should be done and when it should be done and even to prioritize the various items.

Through the years, the To-Do List has proved to be an invaluable and effective Time Management Tool, and many of our most illustrious business Leaders have relied on the List to help them get some very important things done. Here, for example, is Thomas Edison's To-Do List for May 3, 1879:

To-Do List • Thomas Alva Edison

1. Invent first practicable incandescent lamp.

2. Invent phonograph.

3. Create world's first industrial research laboratory.

4. Invent carbon button transmitter.

5. Invent motion picture apparatus.

6. Achieve world record for number of patents filed.

7. Coin memorable phrase for use in future business meetings. (Possibility: Something about the importance of sweat to new product development.)

Gradually, however, as the pace of business has accelerated and the demands on the time of businesspeople have increased, the limitations of the To-Do List have grown more and more apparent.

For example, it can't easily accommodate the constant and rapid changes that may occur in a busy business day. Consider, for example, the To-Do List of a typical businessperson today:

To-Do List • Typical Businessperson

1. Attend long, ineffectual meetings.

2. Eat lunch.

3. Prepare paperwork (shelfware).

4. Rearrange icons on computer desktop.

5. Clip article from business magazine.

6. Reserve golf tee-off time.

And there are other obvious limitations to the To-Do List, including the tendency to crumple and get lost.

Time Management Planners and Systems

In the latter half of the 20th century — in response to the tremendous pressure on our time — a variety of complex systems and protocols have proliferated. In fact, some of these systems can make a religion of Time Management. Unfortunately, as we have seen, none of them have been able to alleviate the most serious Time Management problems — including our disastrous On-Time Start record.

Now a new generation of Time Management Systems is beginning to emerge. These are networked, computer-based systems that incorporate a whole variety of new features and capabilities, organized into a series of layers — each one designed to help the User get the most from his/her time.

Level I: Basic Calendar

The User starts with a simple calendar. Here's what the computer screen (and hard-copy printout) looks like:

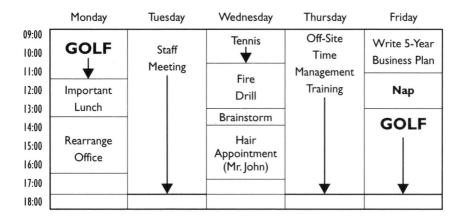

Pretty simple — a typical, busy week with too much to do and not enough time to do it in.

Level IA: Subcalendar

To make the most of each of these appointments, the User can generate a subcalendar, which can be accessed with a single keystroke. For the first few hours of the Staff Meeting, it might look like this:

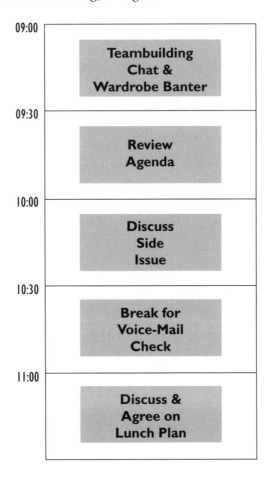

Level IB: Associated Knowledge & Information Windows

Once the calendar item has been broken out in this way, another layer can be added: important associated information that will help the User execute the appointed task. Here, for example, are some of the Knowledge Windows that the User might attach to the Staff Meeting item:

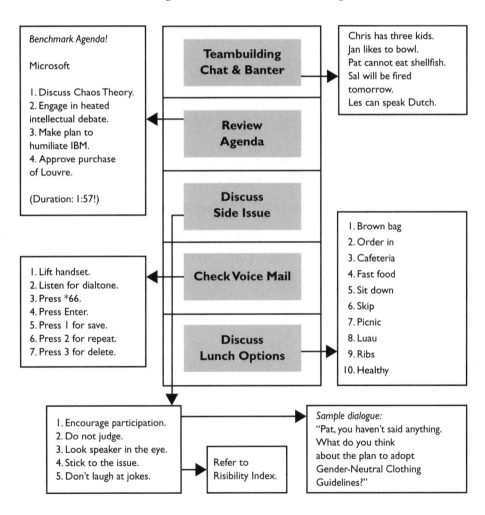

Level II: Filters, Checks, & Alerts

As useful as Level I can be to the individual User, Level II features provide real power to the organization. When the User attempts to enter a To-Do item into his/her personal planner, it is automatically checked against a variety of corporate criteria — mission statement, Critical Success Factors, corporate values, project schedules, budgets, and so forth.

If, for any reason, the item is inconsistent with any of those criteria, it is disallowed and wiped from the screen. At the same time, a Potential Violation Alert (PVA) is transmitted over the network to the appropriate manager, security officer, or regulatory agency.

Level III: Reminders & Prompts

Some organizations have found that even Level II features do not enable their people to fully maximize their time. Accordingly, Level III contains a variety of alarms and mechanical prompts — built in to the User's desktop system — that make it virtually impossible for the User to ignore an approved, scheduled To-Do item. The User can select from:

• Chinese gong/fire horn.

• Recorded reminder from Manager/CEO.

• Inspirational message about the value of time from a well-known expert (call 1-888-4-STHOMAS).

• A "wake-up nozzle" that shoots a harmless jet of ice water into the User's left eye.

Level IV: Behavior Modifiers

Organizations that opt for Level IV Enforcement features have been able to achieve virtually unprecedented time-optimization performance. Level IV recognizes that some employees require extensive behavior modification if they are to improve their Time Management skills. Level IV can be configured with many types of mechanical modifiers.

Two of the most popular are:

☞ **The To-Do Reminder Collar.** Adapted from the highly effective canine no-bark collar, this simple device is permanently fitted to the User. It looks like a bow tie or necklace, but it is programmed to send a stimulating — even refreshing — electrical shock to the User when the time arrives for a scheduled To-Do item. The Collar continues to administer the shock at preprogrammed intervals (generally every three seconds) until the To-Do item has been completed.

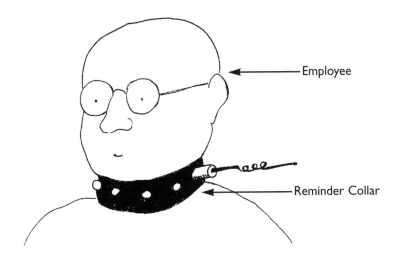

Employee

Reminder Collar

☞ **The Tracking Bracelet.** This Time Management tool has been adapted from the field of law enforcement. The Bracelet — which the User can wear comfortably at all times, thanks to a new, painless, skin-stapling procedure — emits a powerful electronic tone that feeds into the company's Global Positioning System, providing real-time data on the User's position, direction of movement, and ground speed.

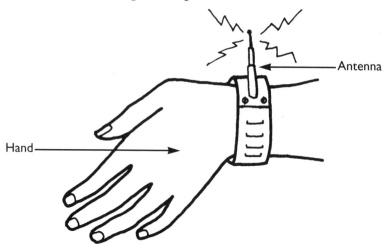

Antenna

Hand

☞ **Nonmechanical Behavior Modifiers.** Some companies, of course, may not consider such mechanical devices to be acceptable in their workplace environments. For these workplaces, Enforcement systems can be purchased with nonmechanical behavior modification tools, including:

- Stocks and Other Public Humiliation Methods.
- Long-Term Psychoanalysis.
- Electroshock.
- Inflatable, Individual Solitary Confinement Cells.

$\mathcal{T}$he Touch Template

Another area in which nonrational human behaviors often disrupt the smooth and controlled flow of business is that of personal relationships: Who likes whom? Who socializes with whom? Who lunches with whom? Who confides in whom? Who is having sexual relations with whom in the executive conference room? Such concerns have a tremendous impact on the productivity and teamworking capability of the workforce.

For the most part, however, these issues of personal relations are simply beyond the ability of the enterprise to analyze and control. But some companies have made a start by focusing on the most tangible and quantifiable manifestation of human relationships: physical touching.

Before I describe these exciting initiatives, let me ask a question:

Q: What would your reaction be if, during a business meeting, a colleague physically touched you?

1. Feel a warm human connection to that colleague.

2. Quickly brush the colleague's hand away and say, "Please, I would prefer not to be touched by you at this time."

3. Report the colleague's behavior to your HR professional.

4. Contact a nationally known business reporter and cooperate in an undercover investigation resulting in a cover story that blows the company sky high.

5. Explain to the colleague that you believe touching should be reserved for nonbusiness hours and suggest a meeting at The Happy Haddock Bar & Grille for, say, 6:15 P.M. on Friday.

Obviously, your answer will depend on a great number of factors, including:

- **Who** the colleague is.
- **Where** you are touched.
- **When** the touch takes place.
- **How** the touch is conducted.

How can touching be better managed in the workplace? One answer is known as The Touch Template. It's an innovative system that enables any organization to create a Touch Policy that is clear, practical, and — best of all — customizable to the prevailing cultural norms.

Here are the elements:

1. The Touch Team. First, the organization creates a Touch Team, generally composed of people from Human Resources, Information Technology, Health Services, and Security.

2. Attitudinal Survey. Next, the Team conducts an Employee Survey of Touching Habits and Attitudes. They ask 432 questions that cover all aspects of touch behavior, including issues such as:

- When is a slap on the butt appropriate?

- How long should a handshake last?

- What do you do if a colleague's foot "bumps" into yours under the conference table?

- Should European men be allowed to kiss American men?

3. Touch Zones. The Team enters the results of the survey — aided by complex software that automatically rectifies and weights the raw data — to create a computer model that defines the Default Touch Zones. The exact dimensions, total number, and designating names of the Touch Zones will be different for each organization. Here's a fairly typical Default Touch Zone model:

Default Touch Zones

Head Area

Upper upper limb

Lower upper limb

Manual Area
(including digits)

Upper lower limb

Lower lower limb

Shod extremities

4. Touch Types. Now The Team creates an index of Standard Touch Types, which catalogs the common kinds of Touching that have been observed or practiced in their particular workplace.

    An icon, or button, is created for each Touch Type that — as we will see — will be used as part of the Touch Template process.

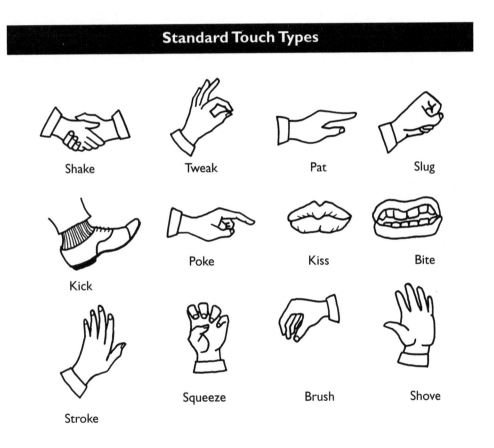

Standard Touch Types

Shake   Tweak   Pat   Slug

Kick   Poke   Kiss   Bite

Stroke   Squeeze   Brush   Shove

5. Touch Parameters. The Team defines a list of Touch Parameters that serve to more closely describe the specific characteristics of the Touch, including Time of Day, Location, Duration of Touch, and Force of Touch (usually measured in pounds per square inch, or PSI).

6. Personal Touch Preferences Profile. Finally, each member of the organization is asked to create his/her own Personal Touch Preferences Profile (PTPP) — which includes restrictions, limitations, and neuroses pertaining to that individual's Touch Zones, Types, and Parameters. Each person is assigned his/her own PTPP ID#.

7. Implementation. The Touch Zones, Types, Parameters, and Profiles are loaded into the Touch Template dedicated High-Performance Server. The computer supports a network of Touch Template Terminals that are placed throughout the facility, usually in such High-Incidence Touch Areas as hallways, meeting rooms, cafeterias, and storage closets.

When a Touch Situation arises, employees proceed to a Terminal where the Windows-based, menu-driven, highly graphical Touch Template User Interface leads them through a simple standard procedure:

Touch Template • Process

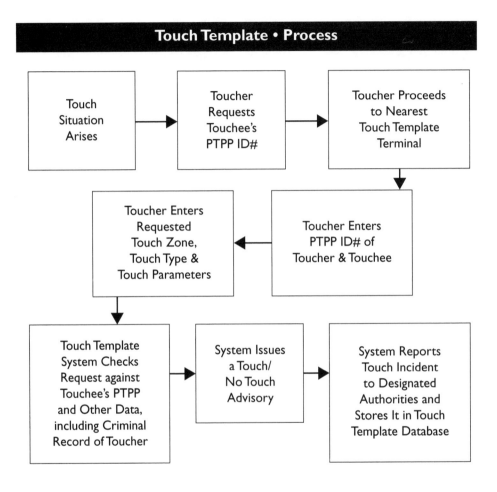

The results of Touch Template usage are still inconclusive. Some people have expressed concern that the system significantly reduces the spontaneity that has long been considered an important part of human Touching. Others, however, say that they feel far more comfortable in the workplace now that Touching has been better quantified.

More time and experience with the Touch Template is needed before its impact on productivity can really be assessed. Meanwhile, the Touch Template is proving, once again, that there is no business issue that cannot be addressed, analyzed, and successfully managed — if the inclination, resources, and technological tools are available.

For your Touch Template system, complete with server, Touch Template terminals, and Touch Zone, Type, Parameter, and Personal Profile software — along with installation, consulting, and training services — call 1-888-4-STHOMAS.

Call 1-888-4-STHOMAS.

*G*ender-Neutral Clothing Guidelines

As an intriguing side note, many organizations have determined that it is more effective to minimize or prevent the number of Touching Incidents than to manage them once they occur — the equivalent of quality control versus quality inspection.

To this end, these companies have focused on the one workplace factor that contributes to the urge to touch more than any other: clothing.

In fact, recent research reveals that clothing style can increase or decrease the Touch Impulse by as much as 86 percent — especially in cases of intergenderal touching.

Accordingly, these companies have developed and enforced innovative Clothing Guidelines designed to minimize the gender-specific physical factors that have proved to contribute to the desire to Touch.

Here are just two examples of this new type of Gender-Neutral Clothing that I have sketched (usually on the backs of envelopes!) in some of the most productive, exciting, and touch-free workplaces around the world:

Everyday Office Wear

This simple, comfortable, everyday outfit features:

- ☛ XXXL midweight tunic-style upper.
- ☛ Calf-length culottes/Casbah bottoms.
- ☛ Nonskid, water-resistant slippers.
- ☛ Unisex briefcase.

Casual Days

Every employee can feel comfortable and correct in this versatile outfit:

- ☛ Lightweight, fully opaque yet breathable Tyvek pajamas.
- ☛ Foot-hugging footwear in durable composite material.

𝓒 all Me Pat

Another method for reducing obvious gender differences may be the most cost-effective of all. It is based on the obvious yet breakthrough realization that a great deal of gender-related affect is contained in a person's *name*, especially the first one.

So, some companies have simply required any employee with a gender-positive name to abandon it and choose a new one from an approved list. We have identified the following first names as particularly effective at minimizing gender:

- Pat   • Chris   • Jan
- Lee   • Sam   • Kim

There can be some inconvenience associated with a workforce comprised of people with just a handful of first names among them. At least one company has overcome the problem by assigning employee numbers, by seniority.

Most organizations have found that employees will easily adapt to being called Pat 37 or Chris 82 if a comprehensive training course in change management is carried out by fully trained Gender Management Professionals.

Call 1-888-4-STHOMAS.

TIME OUT! Where Are *You* Comfortable Being Touched?

Does your comfort with interpersonal touching match that of the average business organization? We polled over 50,000 people in more than 3,000 businesses to determine which Touch Zones they are most comfortable touching on colleagues or having touched on themselves.

We found that, in the great majority of companies, only one Touch Zone was considered totally acceptable, and it was different for men and women:

Most Acceptable Touch Zones

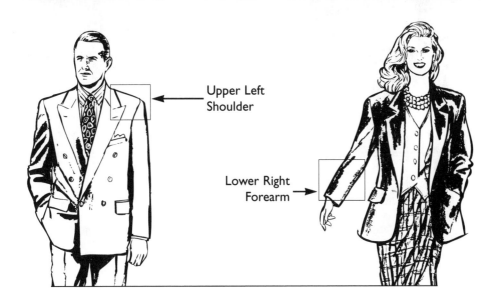

Upper Left Shoulder

Lower Right Forearm

The same poll revealed that there is an equally unacceptable Touch Zone common to all organizations — again differing for men and women:

Least Acceptable Touch Zones

Lips

Upper
Lower
Limb

☞ **EXERCISE:** Now, using the blank male/female Touch Template supplied below, work with your colleagues to determine which are the acceptable/unacceptable Touch Zones in your workgroup or organization.

MALE   **FEMALE**

THE FUTURE IS TOMORROW

"Time is getting shorter.

Speed is getting faster.

*We're arriving at the New Millennium
sooner than was predicted.*

*We're building tomorrow today,
or tomorrow morning at the very latest.*

You're not getting any younger."

STEPHEN MICHAEL PETER THOMAS

Faith-Based Finance

In the future — which is approaching us faster than ever before — all the rules of business are likely to change. But finance is likely to be transformed more than any other activity. Traditional accounting? Gone. Activity-based costing? Gone before it even gets started.

What will take the place of these outmoded and inflexible numbers-based systems?

Faith.

Faith and spirituality.

Faith-Based Finance. Get used to the phrase.

Many have been practicing Faith-Based Finance for years, but one man has emerged as the world's number one proponent of this new movement — Dr. Vree Patchouk.

Dr. Vree, as he is known by his many clients and admirers — and, dare I say it, disciples — lives and works in an unpretentious 39-room Grade I Listed Building with windmill and paddock in the hills west of London.

Join me on a visit to this extraordinary man.

Dr. Vree Patchouk,
leading proponent of
Faith-Based Finance,
works from his office
at his modest home
west of London.

I arrived for my appointment with Dr. Vree at 9:30 A.M. sharp. After being buzzed through the electrified gate, passed through the metal detector, and patted down for concealed weapons, I was ushered into the morning room by Eriche Krauss, the doctor's personal associate (6' 8", Rhodes Scholar, former Mr. World Muscle Detailer, and prize-winning horticulturist), and asked to wait.

Eriche withdrew without offering any refreshment — no mineral water, no fresh fruit, no hazelnut decaf, no single malts — and left me in a room completely empty except for the one Aubusson carpet and a Venetian canalscape by Turner in serious need of cleaning.

Ten minutes passed. Not accustomed to being kept waiting, I considered leaving.

But then, I noticed a pleasant aroma. Sandalwood, I decided. A distant sound caught my attention: I believe it was the discharge of a fowling piece into an innocent game bird.

My senses seemed unusually alert. I remembered a passage from Dr. Vree's best-selling book, *The Five Fundamentals of Financial Freedom*: "Listen to the world, and it will tell you what to do."

So, I listened, carefully. With little effort, I could hear the sound of a butler polishing priceless Asprey silverware in the dining room adjacent. I could hear the voices of workmen as they pulled a high-speed ISDN line through the 18th-century walls to improve Internet response time. And, by placing my ear against the wall, I could hear Dr. Vree talking on the cordless digital telephone in the next room.

"I am loving you, too, and wishing to rub holy ghee upon your yoni," he was saying, obviously to some spiritual adviser of his own.

Next, I turned inward and began to listen deeply to my own most precious thoughts. The first thought that came to mind was, "I wonder how much money this guy makes a year?" This compelling question led me into the following inner dialogue:

> **INNER THOUGHTS:** *Let's say Dr. Vree gets paid $50K a day. Suppose he does 150 gigs a year. That's seven and a half million. He probably pulls in another million in royalties. The merchandise deals could clear another three million at least. Then add in a few directorships, professorships, the stock portfolio, and the odd real estate investment, and the guy's probably pulling in 14 or 15 million a year!*

This dialogue was so intense that I must have blurted out the last few words aloud. As Dr. Vree entered, he smiled and said, "Net!"

And thus began our conversation about how today's organizations are taking a whole new view of finance. Let's listen in...

DR. VREE: Stephen, let us suppose you are the chief executive officer of a company of very high quality.

SMPT: You would like me to vision myself as a CEO?

DR. VREE: Yes, and I am wanting you to suppose that you are wishing very badly to buy a new jet, having inside it leather seatings and an entertainment center that cannot be beat.

Gulfstream V® with leather seatings.

SMPT: Like the Lear 31?

DR. VREE: I was thinking of the Gulfstream V, but the model is immaterial. Now you find yourself facing a familiar prospect, do you not, Stephen?

SMPT: Yes, I'll have to justify this capital expense.

DR. VREE: We are calling it The Moment of Financial Justification. And how will you go about creating such a justification?

SMPT: I suppose I'll task my staff to do a complete analysis of comparative costs and projected return on investment.

DR. VREE: But you and I are knowing that these complicated numbers do not matter a parcel.

SMPT: What do you mean?

DR. VREE: Because you will buy the jet if you truly believe the jet should be bought.

SMPT: You're saying that belief is a better justification than traditional ROI analysis?

DR. VREE: Yes, you must have faith that the jet will improve your business. Because, if you have faith, it will. If you do not, it won't.

SMPT: Okay, but jets are a special case. What about other types of expenditure?

DR. VREE: The bigger the expense, the more faith you must have. Those who build huge buildings, those who install great worldwide computer networks, those who send satellites up into the sky — these are people of the greatest faith.

SMPT: But what about my board of directors? What if they don't share my belief?

DR. VREE: You must try to help them share your belief. In the case of the jet, you might perhaps take them for a short test flight. Serve hot canapés and Taittinger flower bottle champagne, and explain that the jet could sometimes be available for their own personal use.

SMPT: And if that doesn't work?

DR. VREE: Then you must try to teach by metaphor. You might say to them, "Justifying the cost of a jet is not unlike justifying the cost of a director like you. To some shareholders, your annual fees, first-class travel expenses, and other perquisites might be difficult to justify for a position that requires attendance at only ten meetings a year. But you and I know that it is impossible to put a price on the counsel and wisdom of a fine member of the board. Well, the same is true of the Gulfstream V. You cannot put a price on soaring through the sky in leather seatings."

SMPT: And this will work?

DR. VREE: Oh yes, it will work, Stephen. It works, if you believe it works.

There's more to Faith-Based Finance, much more. And you can start your Learning the very next time you need to justify a large capital expense. Simply spend less time on the numbers and more time in helping others share your belief.

How can you do that?

Listen to the world. It will tell you what to do.

*M*ental Modeling
for the New Millennium

Beyond Faith-Based Finance, what will the workplace of the future look like? How will your company be functioning in the years ahead?

The best way to control the future of your company is to create a mental model of how you want it to be, and then work to create it.

Some of our most successful Leaders — from political heavyweights to corporate giants — say they have achieved their results through Mental Modeling.

SAM WALTON: MASS RETAILING AS CROSS-COUNTRY SKIING

Most people know that the legendary (now deceased, alas!) Sam Walton was a workaholic, pilot, quality fanatic, ceaseless traveler, and fabulously rich. But few know that his Mental Model for the future of automated mass retailing was cross-country skiing.

In fact, I was there when he developed the model. It was the winter of 1989, and I had arranged to spend three days with the Old Retailer, meeting him in Farup, North Dakota, and flying with him in his private aircraft, watching him in action and Learning his secrets of supply-chain management.

The day before we were to take off, seven feet of snow fell in Farup. The Farup airport wasn't just closed, it couldn't even be located. But do you think a mere 84 inches of snow could stop the Patriarchal Billionaire from making his customary rounds from store to store? Before I knew it, Sam and I were gliding along on brand new pairs of ArtiConquerer Feather-Lite, Titani-Comp, X-Country Skis (available in bulk at a 20 percent discount at Sam's Club).

Unfortunately, before we were more than a few miles out, I lost my footing (due no doubt to a faulty binding) and slid into the Nation's Number One Discounter. He lost his balance, careered off the trail, and crashed through the ice and into the frigid waters of a frozen creek.

I hurried to Sam's side and fished him out by his gaiters. Cold, but undaunted, Sam dried himself off and insisted that we continue on. "It's only forty-five miles to Wal-Mart Store #126!" he exhorted. "They're running a coupon promotion on Robitussin® DM with a special 3-D end-cap display that we can't miss!" he exclaimed with characteristic enthusiasm. "Promotion ends Tuesday. No rain checks!"

Alas, by nightfall, Sam was in the grip of a severe chill as a result of his unplanned dip into the creek and couldn't ski a furlong farther. I started a fire with one of the E-Z Lite Multi-Color WeekEnder Fireplace Logs (six for $3.99) that Sam had brought along and made the Former 5&10 Franchiser as comfortable as I could in his SnuggleDown Velcrite CampBag Sleeper (some slightly irregular). Even after a hearty meal of Dinty Moore Lo-Fat Irish Stew (in the 72-ounce Family Pak), accompanied by a steaming 16-ounce Thermo-Mug of Flu-Be-Gone Medicated Hot Drink, Sam continued to weaken. By midnight, he had lapsed into delirium.

I realized it was up to me to bring the Pioneer of HyperMarketing home alive — the nation's economy was depending on me. So, I did the only thing I could do. I crawled into the SnuggleDown Sleeper with Sam, took him in my arms, and began to talk business. I prattled on about the evolution of business management thought, about value chain strategies, about the differences between the multinational and global corporation, and about how the growth of large retailers was affecting the performance of their now-smaller suppliers.

Sam seemed to gain strength from the richness and provocativeness of my ideas. Soon, although delirious, he jumped into the dialogue. That night I believe we invented the discipline of Mental Modeling. We created a parallel between our situation — cross-country skiers, lost, with their survival in question — and the future of automated mass retailing.

Not only did it save our lives that frigid night, the Model we created established a new course for Wal-Mart that would eventually lead to intense confrontations with state and local authorities in the states of Maine, Massachusetts, New Hampshire, and Vermont. But that's another story.

Sam, focused even in his delirium, first addressed the issue of corporate mission. "The Track," he screamed, "we have to find the right Track!" He thrashed this way and that, as if looking for the best route to take through the Forest of Possibilities that confront every retailer.

"No, no! Not that way! We'll die that way!" he screamed, clutching me and pointing back the way we had come. I realized that he must be constructing an elaborate competitive paradigm and that each "track" through the woods represented a different business strategy to his febrile but still perceptive mind.

"No, we won't go that way," I said, thinking quickly. "No, because that way is the Lo-Cost, Lo-Valu, Lo-Service, Lo-Inventory trail. Sears went that way. And K-Mart before them. And Ames and Bradlees. You're right, Sam, disaster waits at the end of that trail!"

He lurched up. "We can't go that way because there's a Cold Dark Creek back there! You nearly killed me!"

"You're right. A Cold Dark Creek of Chapter Eleven status!" I agreed. "And maybe even a rushing torrent of hostile takeover," I elaborated.

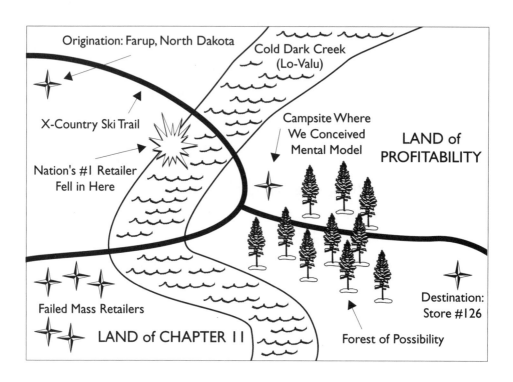

"We can't go that way," he begged once more, then lapsed into a fevered babbling that jumbled up warehousing and delivery vehicles and 15-day invoicing.

After several hours of rambling, Sam turned lucid again. His eye fell on the gleaming titanium binding of my ski. "You didn't have your bindings on properly," he shrieked. "You had your right ski on your left foot! That's why you slipped and nearly killed me!"

I realized that Sam was again elaborating on this complex Model that was forming in his mind. He was not really talking about my binding as a binding at all, but as a metaphor for inventory control. "You have to keep the toes tight when you're skiing!" he screamed. "Yes," I agreed, easily making the connection between bindings and retailing. "Yes, you need absolute control over your inventory all along the supply chain — you have to keep those connections extremely tight."

"But your heels should be loose!" he moaned. "You mean," I translated, "that you must also be flexible enough to respond to market demand."

"Only an idiot puts the left ski on the right foot," Sam said weakly, before slipping into a fitful sleep.

"You're right, Sam," I told him, placing a cool hand on his burning brow. I puzzled for some time over what he meant by "idiot" and realized, at last, that Sam was referring to his Luddite competitors who had been ineffectual at implementing automated inventory systems.

I think you can see how effective Mental Modeling can be. I'm happy to say that Sam was fit as a fiddle the next morning and we reached store #126 in time for what proved to be a very healthy Robitussin promotion.

Although you may have heard Sam disavow his role in developing the Mental Model Method — or of ever skiing with me — I think that's just his characteristic modesty.

For your Mental Modeling Starter Kit — complete with some of the metaphors developed by our most successful businesspeople — call 1-888-4-STHOMAS. Kits available in Religion, Family, or the popular Sports Metaphor versions.

Call 1-888-4-STHOMAS.

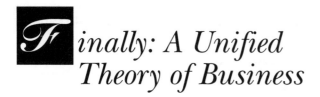 inally: A Unified Theory of Business

In this chapter, I shall attempt to do what no other business writer has accomplished before: bring the Learnings of the ages (and the gurus) together into a Unified Theory of Business.

Too often, business writers and theorists explore a limited set of Learnings, leaving the already beleaguered businessperson to integrate and assimilate the many disparate Learnings available. Consider the vast supply of ideas and concepts, principles and laws, strategies and practices, disciplines and habits promulgated through books and tapes and seminars and training sessions and, most important, merchandise. And, of course, not all of these ideas agree!

As you well know, in today's fast-paced competitive world of global business, few people can afford to spend time thinking, let alone devoting the heavy mind-time it takes to create a highly integrated, fully practicable Unified Theory. So, I have done it for you.

We start with the essential element of the Unified Theory: the **individual businessperson**. You! You are at the center of your universe, just as I am at the center of mine. (Although mine may be significantly larger and more important than yours, that doesn't matter!) Here you are:

Unified Theory #1 • The Individual Businessperson — You!

Next, every individual has specific personal needs. Even if we feel some modicum of loyalty to our organization, our first allegiance will always be to ourselves and those fundamental **needs**. Here they are:

Unified Theory #2 • Individual Needs

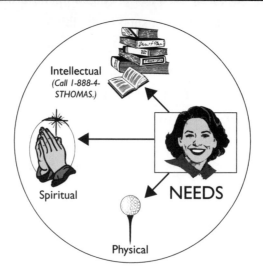

At the same time, each individual should set real and attainable **goals**. For businesspeople, these goals are generally achievable only through an organization of some kind. Here's what the goals might look like:

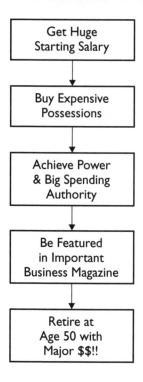

Unified Theory #3 • Goals

Get Huge
Starting Salary

↓

Buy Expensive
Possessions

↓

Achieve Power
& Big Spending
Authority

↓

Be Featured
in Important
Business Magazine

↓

Retire at
Age 50 with
Major $$!!

Now, these individual Needs and Goals must be pursued within the context of the variety of **responsibilities** that each Individual shoulders to a variety of entitites:

Unified Theory #4 • Responsibilities

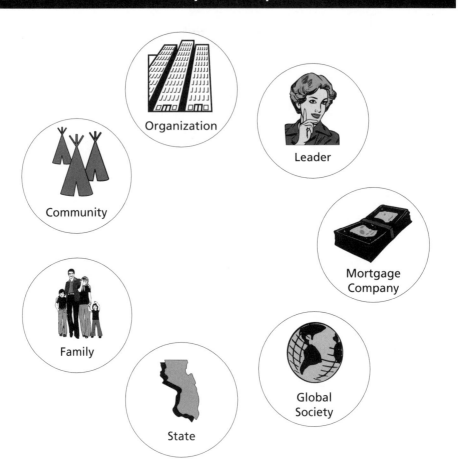

Then, of course, you must carry out these responsibilities according to a set of **principles** and beliefs that both the organization and you, as an individual, share. For example:

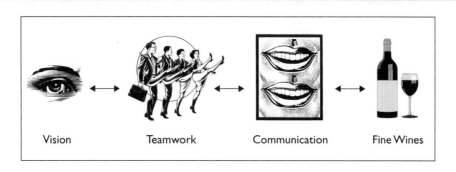

Next, of course, you must realize that no organization operates autonomously. The company is but one link in a **value chain** that begins with raw material and ends with a high-quality product that the consumer wishes to purchase:

Now, add your organizational Smeaton-Thomas Success Factors Grid…

Unified Theory #7 • Business Success Factors

	Bad	Good
Fast	Fast & Bad	**Fast** *&* **Good!**
Slow	Slow & Bad	Slow & Good

…and all that's left is to add your organizational mission statement, specific relevant business strategy, 12-month tactics, financial objectives, and operating budgets, and you've got it!

Put it all together and it looks like this: The Thomas Unified Theory of Business — at last!!

I wish you every success in applying it to your business!

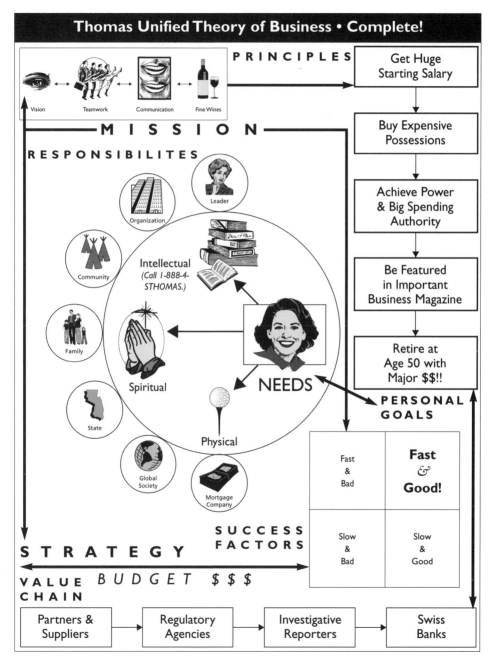

Thomas Unified Theory of Business • Complete!

PRINCIPLES

Vision — Teamwork — Communication — Fine Wines

MISSION

RESPONSIBILITES

Organization
Leader
Community
Intellectual
(Call 1-888-4-STHOMAS.)
Family
Spiritual
State
Physical
Global Society
Mortgage Company

NEEDS

Get Huge
Starting Salary

Buy Expensive
Possessions

Achieve Power
& Big Spending
Authority

Be Featured
in Important
Business Magazine

Retire at
Age 50 with
Major $$!!

PERSONAL
GOALS

Fast & Bad	**Fast & Good!**
Slow & Bad	Slow & Good

SUCCESS
FACTORS

STRATEGY

VALUE CHAIN   *BUDGET $ $ $*

| Partners & Suppliers | Regulatory Agencies | Investigative Reporters | Swiss Banks |

A Note of Caution

Before buying or using any business book, be sure to check the credentials and qualifications of its author.

> *We have received reports, for example, of an obscure "author" (whose name I will not dignify by mentioning) who has written a business book "satire."*

This might be an innocuous — even amusing — activity, except that it has come to our attention that thousands of unsuspecting readers, eager to learn and improve, have taken this work as legitimate. In fact, many have attempted to implement this "author's" so-called "ideas" — sometimes with disastrous results.

If you come across this impostor's work, please, consume it in the spirit of fun in which it was meant.

> *Do not attempt to implement any of his phony principles or practices in your workplace or in your home. If you do, I doubt that even this book,* **The Book That's Sweeping America!***, can provide a remedy.*

So, please, do as so many of the world's most influential business leaders have done...

…choose your Guru wisely!

TOOLS FOR FURTHER LEARNING

STEPHEN MICHAEL PETER THOMAS

Read Me! *Before* You Begin Implementing These Learnings

First, let me thank you for reading (or skimming, or at least holding in your hands) this book.

You have Learned a great deal. But now the challenging part begins: Implementation. Before you set about creating change in your organization based upon these Learnings, please remember the following:

☛ You — and everyone within your organization — must fully, totally, completely, and unreservedly commit to the scrupulous application of the Learnings. If you don't, the Learnings will have no effect whatsoever.

☛ You must discard all other Learnings from all other consultants, gurus, and advisers and devote 100 percent of your time and energy to implementing The Thomas Learnings. If you don't, they will have little or no effect whatsoever.

☛ You must realize that it might take years (possibly decades) to achieve any noticeable results with the Learnings. Even when you do achieve a result, you may not be able to attribute it to the Learning — or you may be unable to measure it in any meaningful way.

☛ In fact, you may never achieve any result at all. If that is the case, studies show that it is not the fault of the Learning itself. Rather, it is because you have failed to understand the Learning properly, implemented it incorrectly, or failed to make a total commitment to it.

But, don't be discouraged or alarmed! There are several steps you can take to pave the way for change throughout your organization and significantly improve your chances of achieving results within your lifetime. Here they are:

1. Place your copy of *The Book That's Sweeping America!* in a prominent position on your office credenza.

2. Order copies of *The Book That's Sweeping America!* for every member of your organization. (Bulk rates available. Call 1-888-4-STHOMAS.)

3. Restructure your review-and-reward system to make purchase and reading of *The Book That's Sweeping America!* mandatory.

4. Require that every member of every supplier, partner, and strategic ally has read *The Book That's Sweeping America!* and demonstrates the ability to conduct business in the spirit of the Learnings before you will do any further business with them.

5. Offer a copy of *The Book That's Sweeping America!* as a premium or incentive to every client or customer. Our Consultants are standing by to assist you in developing innovative packaging and promotional solutions.

6. Open a Thomas Learnings Center to provide Thomas merchandise in every company facility. A wide range of point-of-sale materials is available, including display units, end cappers, shelf talkers, and spring-loaded rack mounts.

7. Carry *The Book That's Sweeping America!* with you at all times, including speaking engagements or media interviews, and refer to it often. When showing it, be sure to hold it high and — when appearing on television — at a slight angle to the lights to avoid glare.

Please let us know how you have integrated The Thomas Learnings into your business organization — we'd love to hear from you! (Sorry, no collect calls, please!)

*T*homas Learning Tools & Implementation Products

We are pleased to offer an extensive family of Learning Tools and Implementation Products, just a few of which are listed here. Each Thomas Tool is carefully designed — and fully field-tested — to help facilitate the application of the ideas in this book to your workplace.

All proceeds from the sale of these products are donated to The Thomas Foundation to support further research in the field of business management and the costly first-class travel that it requires.

For the full catalog, containing over 175 high-quality Learning Tools and Implementation Products — ranging from virgin vinyl notebook dividers to an AV-enabled, 38-seat bus for off-site Leadership Conferences — please call **1-888-4-STHOMAS.**

☞ **Smeaton-Thomas Success Factors Grid® Kit**

	Bad	**Good**
Fast	Fast & Bad	**Fast** *&* **Good!**
Slow	Slow & Bad	Slow & Good

Each kit contains:

• 5,000 blank Smeaton-Thomas Success Factors Grid pads, in various sizes.

• User's Guide (592 pages, illustrated).

• 500 Model Grids, many applicable to your business (including those shown in this book).

• 5 free hours in the Smeaton-Thomas Success Factors Grid Web Site Chat-room.

☞ The Touch Template

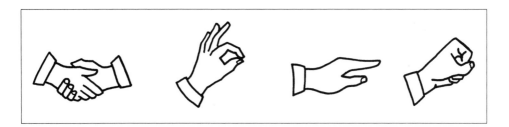

Each system includes:

- 1 client-server computer network, with High-Performance Server.
- The Touch Template Terminal.
- System Documentation (1 CD-ROM, or 498-page booklet).
- 47 hours system consultation.
- 3 hours free legal representation.

☞ **Annals of Time Management Series: To-Do Lists of the World's Most Succesful People**

> *1. Invent first practicable incandescent lamp.*
>
> *2. Invent phonograph.*
>
> *3. Create world's first industrial research laboratory.*
>
> *4. Invent carbon button transmitter.*
>
> *5. Invent motion picture apparatus.*
>
> *6. Achieve world record for number of patents filed.*
>
> *7. Coin memorable phrase for use in future business meetings. (Possibility: Something about the importance of sweat to new product development.)*

This collection of actual To-Do Lists of some of our most successful and influential business and political Leaders provides useful models for you to follow in organizing your *own* activities for the day. Learn how these luminaries prioritized their schedules and how they ensured that what they *planned* to do, they actually *did*. Series includes the To-Do Lists of Eli Whitney (the day he invented the cotton gin), Eleanor Roosevelt, Henry Ford (the day he got the idea for the assembly line), George Washington Carver, Oprah Winfrey, Bill Gates (the day he sold DOS to IBM), and many many others.

☞ The Thomas Line of Gender-Neutral Clothing

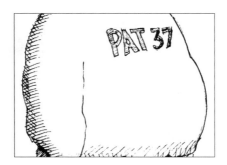

Current Gender-Neutral items available include:

• Culottes (no-fly, elastic waistband).

• No-see-thru pajamas.

• Ergonomic flip-flops.

• XXXL tunic-style upper. Available with the following gender-neutral names embroidered on chest:

> • Pat
> • Chris
> • Jan
> • Lee
> • Sam
> • Kim
> • Bobby
> • Les

☛ Founding Environments® Air Scents

Lost the magic of the early days of your enterprise? Well, if you can't move headquarters back into the garage, you *can* bring back its distinctive scent. Simply spray one of these aromas in the air — or pump them through your HVAC system — and let the powerful pheromones stimulate business results you haven't experienced since those days of 100 percent growth!

Comes in four sizes: Pencil Drawer Sachet, Briefcase Atomizer, Division-Size Drum, or Tank Car.

Scents available:
- Garage
- Barn
- Chicken coop
- Car
- Basement
- Kitchen

Europe only:
- Stately home
- Abattoir
- Canal barge

☞ New Product Development Kit

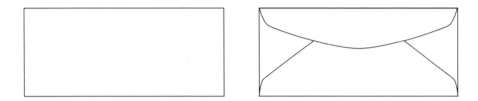

Take advantage of the simplest, yet most effective New Product Development Tool the world has ever known: the Envelope. Inventors and engineers from Leonardo to Thomas Edison have relied on the Envelope to record their inspirations — swiftly, simply, and conveniently.

Each kit includes:

• 20,000 smooth-finish, brite-white, no-tear Number 10 Envelopes.
• 500 Inspirational Envelopes, containing intriguing but unfinished designs for products the world has long clamored for, including the perpetual motion machine, 3-D transmission devices, and the low-cost, solar-powered auto.
• 1,000 pencil stubs, crayons, dried-up markers, and leaky ballpoints of the type favored by engineers.

☞ **The Illustrated Guide to Global Hand Gestures and Facial Expressions**

Each kit contains everything you need to Learn this Global Communication System and to Teach others in your organization, including:

• Interactive CD-ROM. With this computer-based Training Tool, you'll master the Global Gestures without having to leave your desktop!

• Train the Trainer Flash Cards. This deck of illustrated cards tucks neatly into your briefcase so you can take it with you on the Concorde or the TGV or while riding a camel!

To order,
or for complete catalog,
call 1-888-4-STHOMAS.
MBAs & CEO-Level Consultants
standing by 24x365!

The Stephen Michael Peter Thomas Communication & Transportation Signature Collection

☛ **The Stephen Michael Peter Thomas Limited Edition Hummer®
Off-Road Vehicle and Mobile Conference Center**

(Courtesy: Hummer)

Transport your team through any terrain in this virtually invincible 4WD industrial-strength vehicle. Comes equipped with:

- Global Positioning System (GPS) for No-Directions-Needed driving.
- Pop-up Satellite Dish with full sports programming package.
- Full set of Stephen Michael Peter Thomas audio tapes.
- Golf clubs and full-sized, stowaway golf cart.
- Wet bar, pants presser.
- Leather seating areas.
- Stephen Michael Peter Thomas signature painted on hood and mudguards.
- And more!

☞ The Stephen Michael Peter Thomas Limited Edition Gulfstream V Corporate Jet

(Courtesy: Gulfstream)

The coveted GV aircraft quickly climbs to 45,000 feet and soars above congested airways and turbulence, while its 100-percent-fresh-air cabin delivers you to your destination rested and refreshed.

Limited Edition comes equipped with:
- Global Positioning System (GPS) for No-Directions-Needed flying.
- Full set of Stephen Michael Peter Thomas audio and video tapes.
- Leather seating areas.
- Fully licensed pilot and co-pilot.
- Stephen Michael Peter Thomas signature on rudder, flaps, and wing tanks.

☞ The Stephen Michael Peter Thomas Limited Edition StarTAC™ Wearable Cellular Phone

(Courtesy: Motorola)

This is the cell phone that Stephen Michael Peter Thomas chooses for his personal use. The smallest, the lightest, the *coolest* phone on the market. The Stephen Michael Peter Thomas edition comes with Steve's signature on the antenna as well as embossed on the leatherette holster.

$\mathcal{S}$uggested Readings

If you've enjoyed this book, you may wish to read my earlier books:

Anything You Can Do, I Can Do Better. Copy Cop, 1989.

The Anything You Can Do, I Can Do Better Fieldbook. Kinko's, 1991.

There are, of course, other writers on business and related subjects whose works are worth scanning, if not actually reading, including:

The Prince. Niccolò Machiavelli (1469–1527). Excellent advice should you need to conquer a nation-state.

An Inquiry into the Nature and Causes of the Wealth of Nations. Adam Smith (1723–1790). I am a firm believer in Smith's ideas about self-interest.

Seven Habits of Highly Effective People. Stephen Covey. I consider Covey an important role model, especially because of the extensive range of merchandise he offers.

In Pursuit of Wow! Tom Peters. In this book, Tom Peters makes the transition from management evangelist to impassioned graphic designer.

Reengineering the Corporation. Michael Hammer and James Champy. Hammer is the funniest stand-up comedian in the business.

Goodbye!

*Thank you for
Learning with me!*

☛ For further information about the "ideas" of Stephen Michael Peter Thomas, or to inquire about his market-leading fees for consulting or speaking engagements, please contact:

1-888-4-STHOMAS
(toll-free voice line)

STHOMAS.com
(E-mail)

Stephen Michael Peter Thomas
306 Dartmouth Street
Boston, MA 02116
(mail)

Index

Credits

Book Design

Diego Vainesman

Illustration

(In order of appearance)

Wilson's Fish Sign, Glenn Palmer-Smith

Wilson's Fish Org. Chart, Glenn Palmer-Smith

John Smeaton's Gridde, Glenn Palmer-Smith

Bomb Squad, Pamela Prichett

Hot Coal, Pamela Prichett

Big Ship, Pamela Prichett

Diner, Pamela Prichett

Tire, Pamela Prichett

Telling a Joke, Glenn Palmer-Smith

Presenting a Joke, Glenn Palmer-Smith

The Wheel, Glenn Palmer-Smith

The Sandwich, Glenn Palmer-Smith

String-on-Finger, Pamela Prichett

String-on-Finger Archiving, Glenn Palmer-Smith

To-Do Reminder Collar, Glenn Palmer-Smith

Tracking Bracelet, Pamela Prichett

Standard Touch Types, Pamela Prichett

Everyday Office Wear, Glenn Palmer-Smith

Casual Days, Glenn Palmer-Smith

Photography

(In order of appearance)

Stephen Michael Peter Thomas (all photos), Gordon Munro

Lee Iacocca, Corbis-Bettmann

Bill Gates, Reuters/Corbis-Bettmann

Margaret Thatcher, Reuters/Corbis-Bettmann

Ray Wilson, Sherman Hines/Masterfile

Egypt: Sacrifice to God Honus, Corbis-Bettmann

Bomb Squad, UPI/Corbis-Bettmann

Colin Powell, UPI/Corbis-Bettmann

Arnold Palmer, UPI/Corbis-Bettmann

Don King, UPI/Corbis-Bettmann

Karl Marx, Corbis-Bettmann

Madonna, Reuters/Corbis-Bettmann

Jesse Jackson, UPI/Corbis-Bettmann

Al Gore, UPI/Corbis-Bettmann

Boris Yeltsin, Reuters/Corbis-Bettmann

Founding Environment, John Butman

Blenheim Palace, Corbis-Bettmann

Gulfstream V Jet, Gulfstream

Ross Perot, UPI/Corbis-Bettmann

Photomontage

Planet Interactive